FOR ALL MY WRITERS.
WITHOUT YOU NONE
OF THIS WOULD BE
POSSIBLE.

JOHN STRAWN
FOUNDER

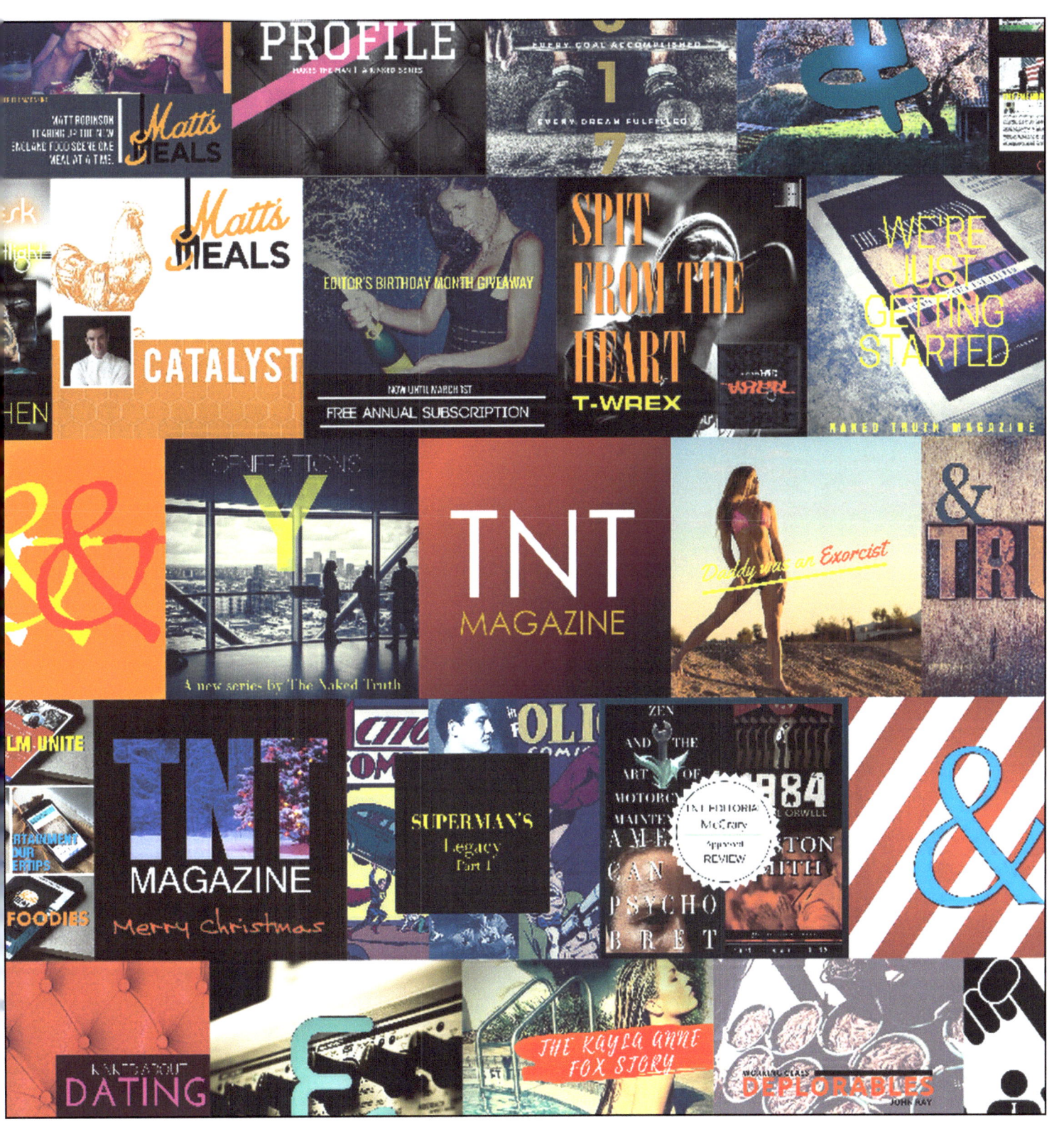

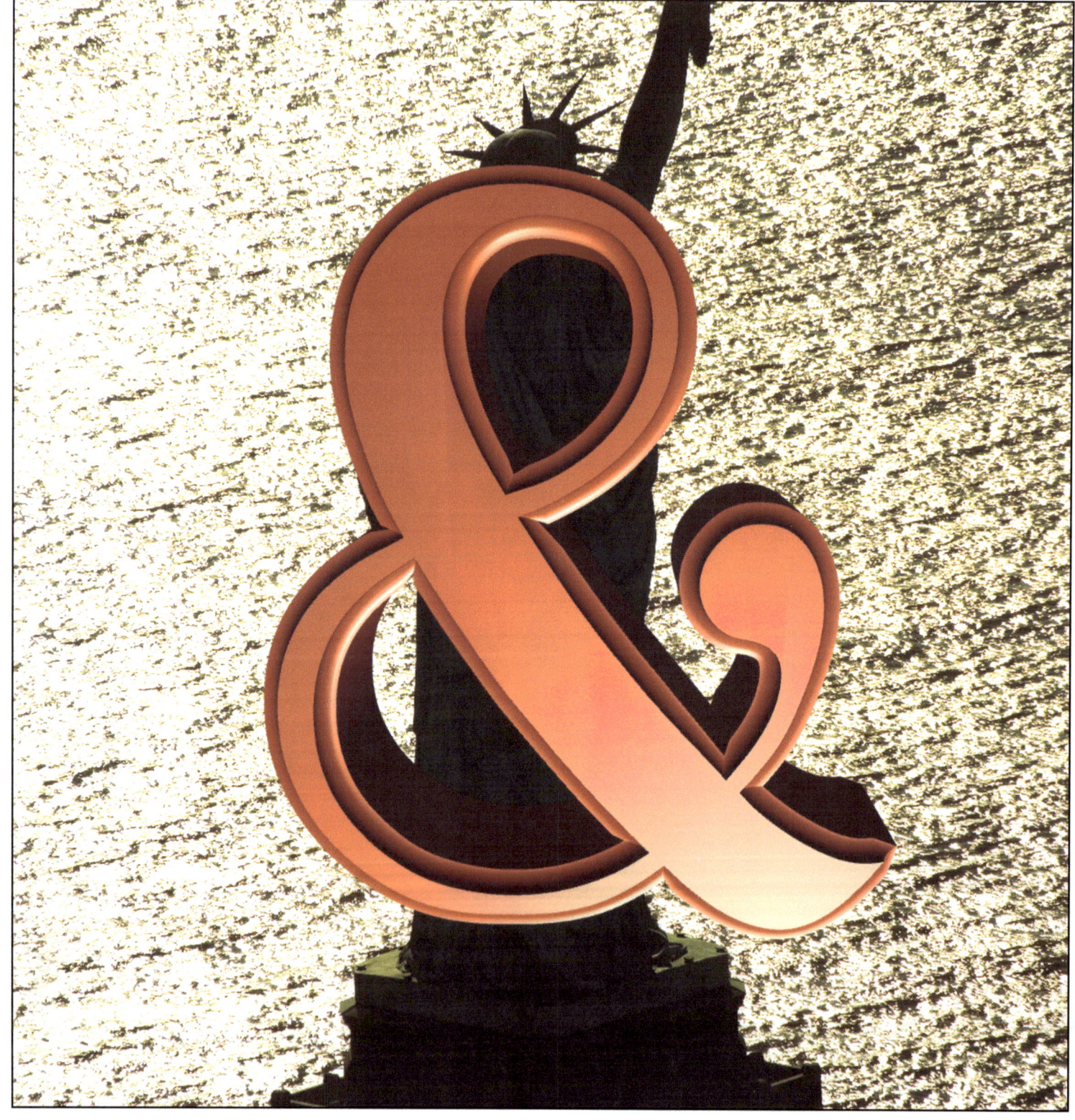

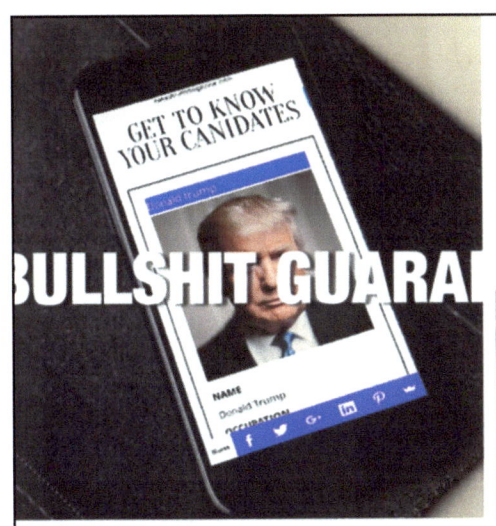

BULLSHIT GUARAI

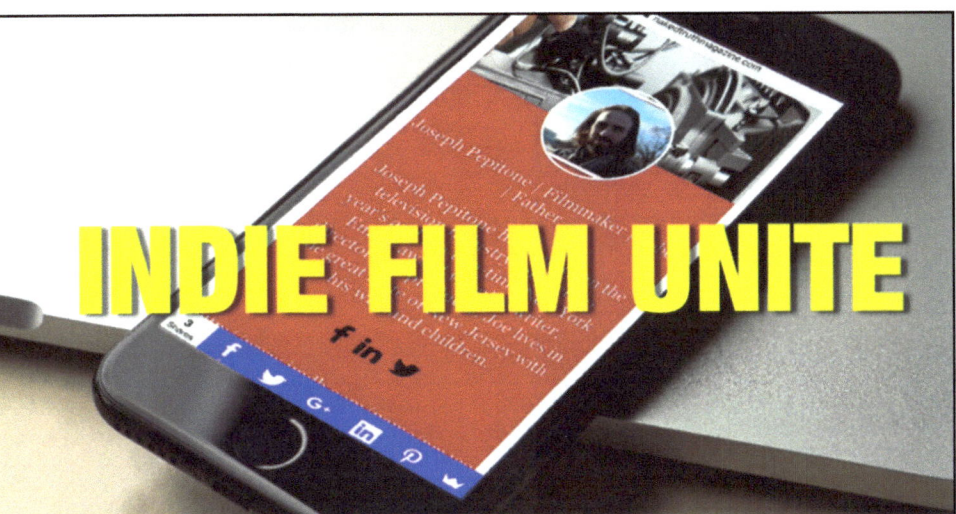

INDIE FILM UNITE

MUSIC

FILM

ART

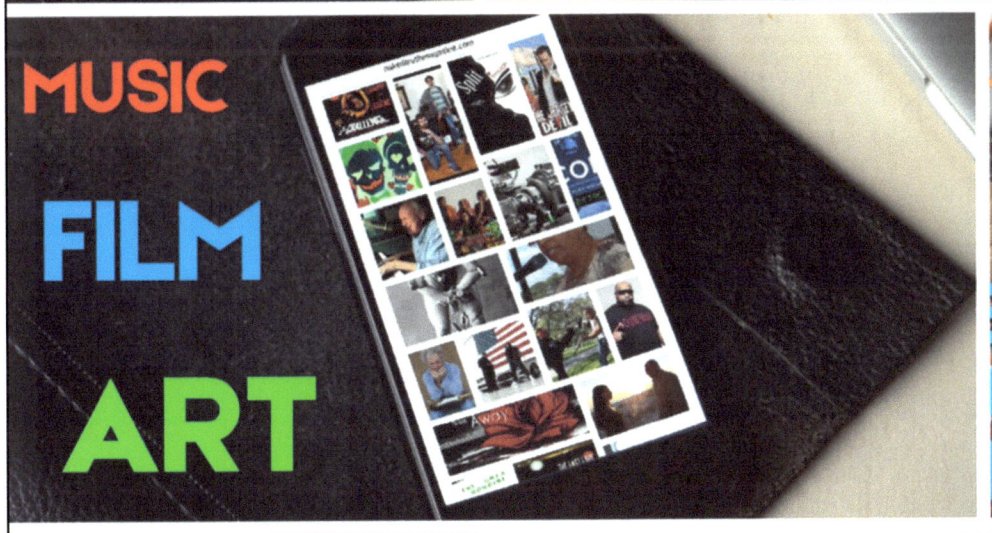

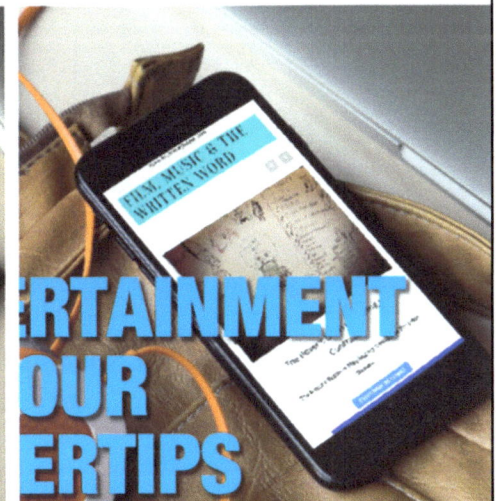

ERTAINMENT
OUR
ERTIPS

YRE
CAL
T

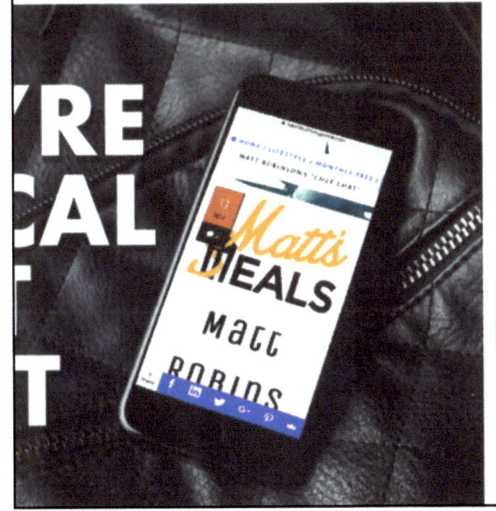

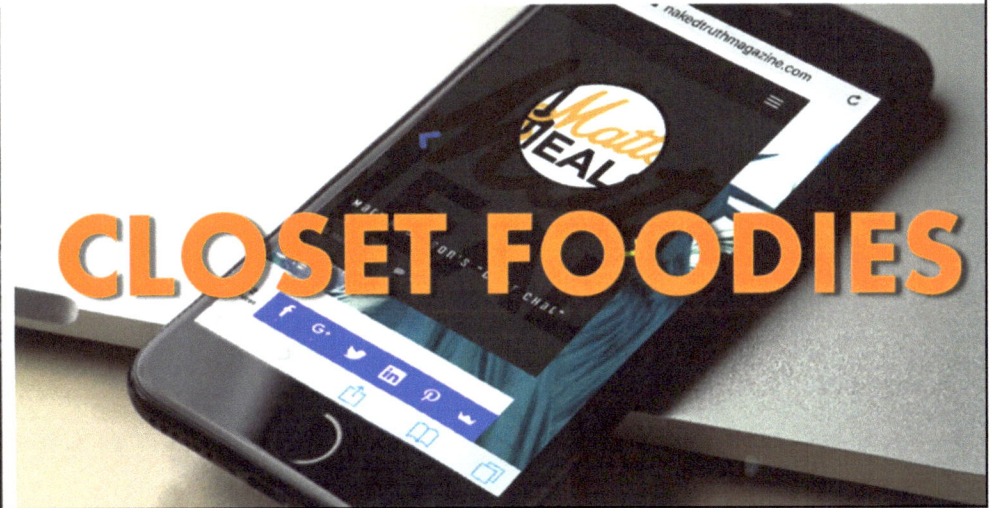

CLOSET FOODIES

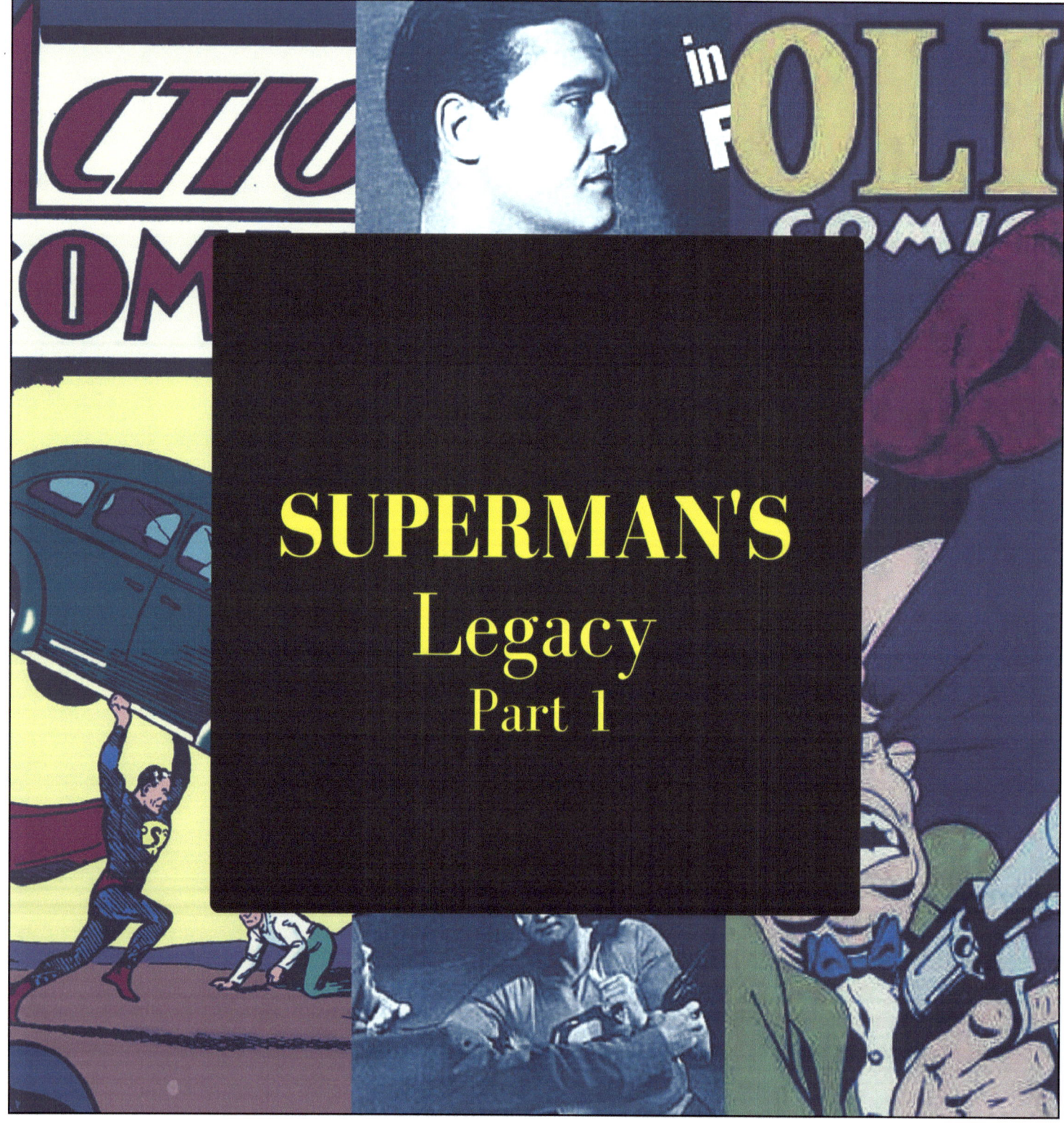

# SUPERMAN'S
## Legacy
### Part 1

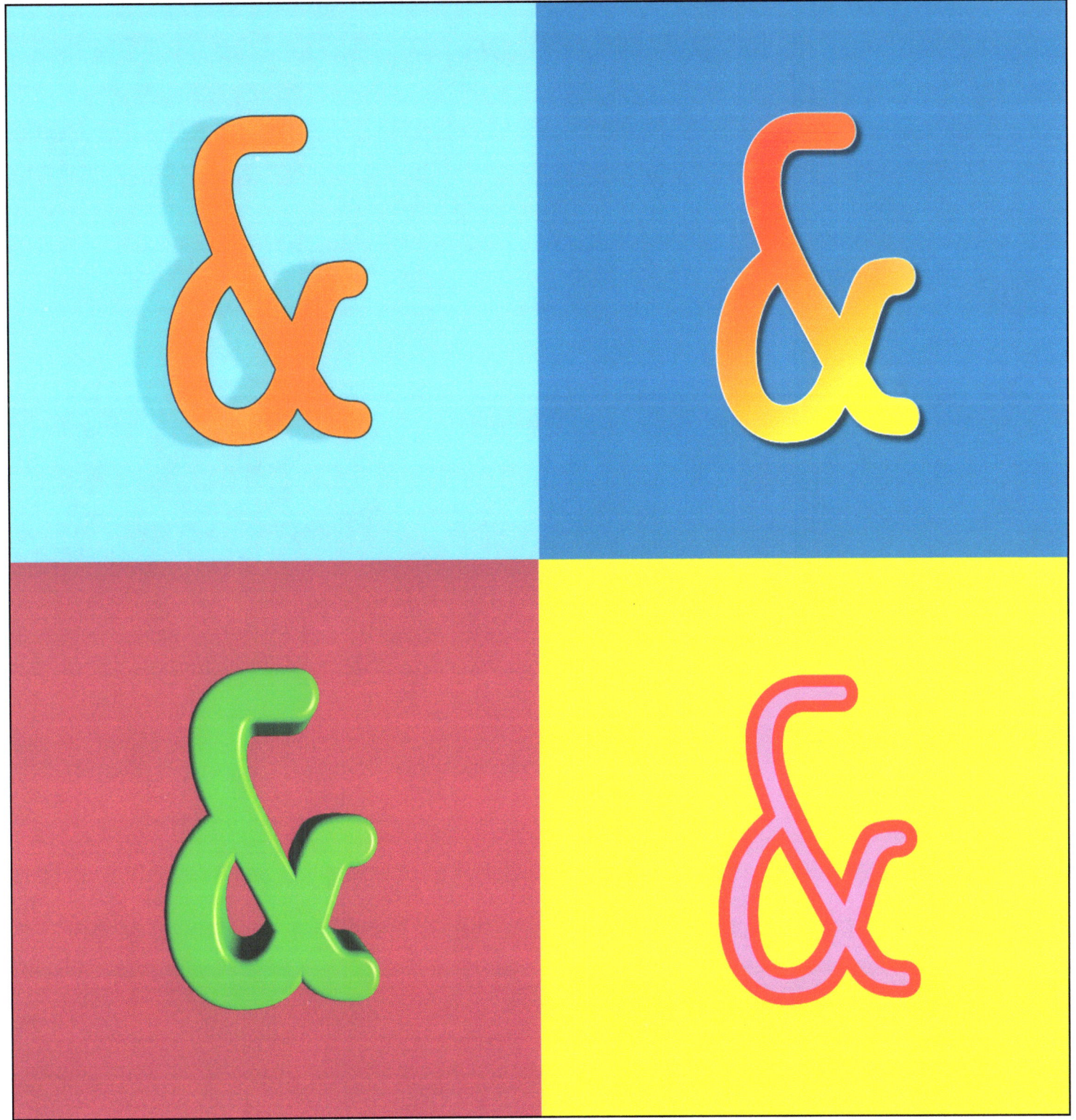

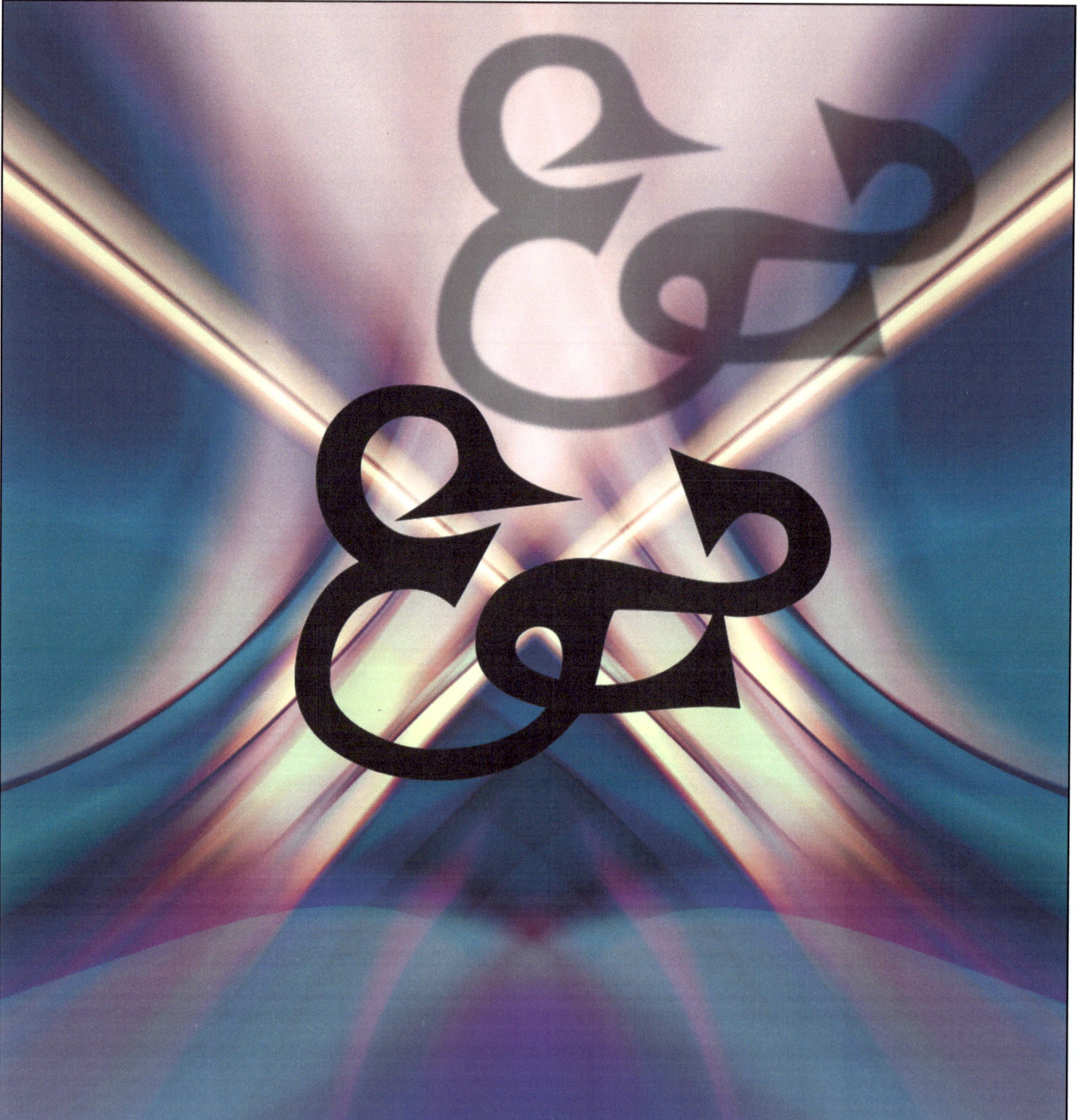

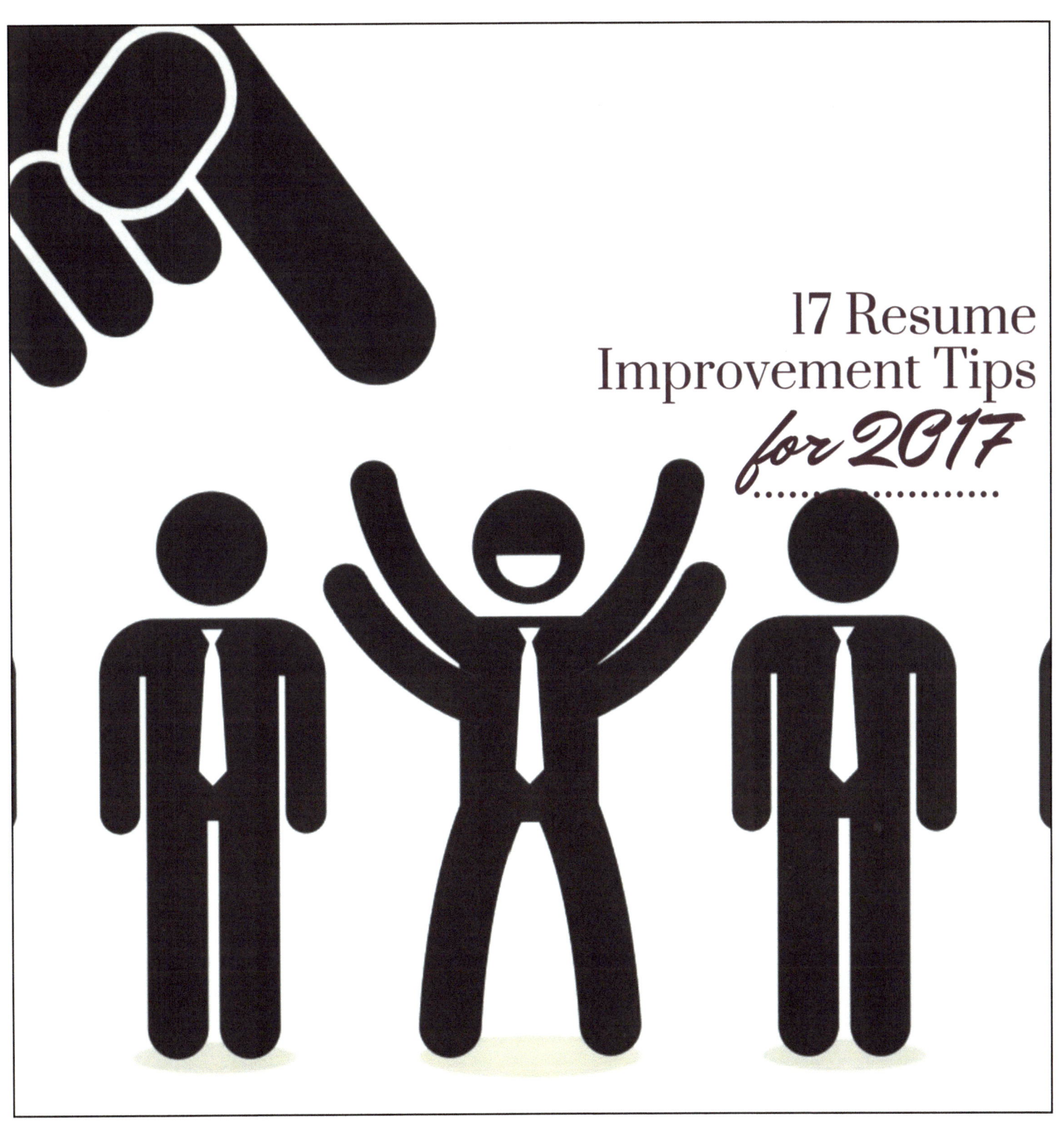

# 17 Resume Improvement Tips
## for 2017

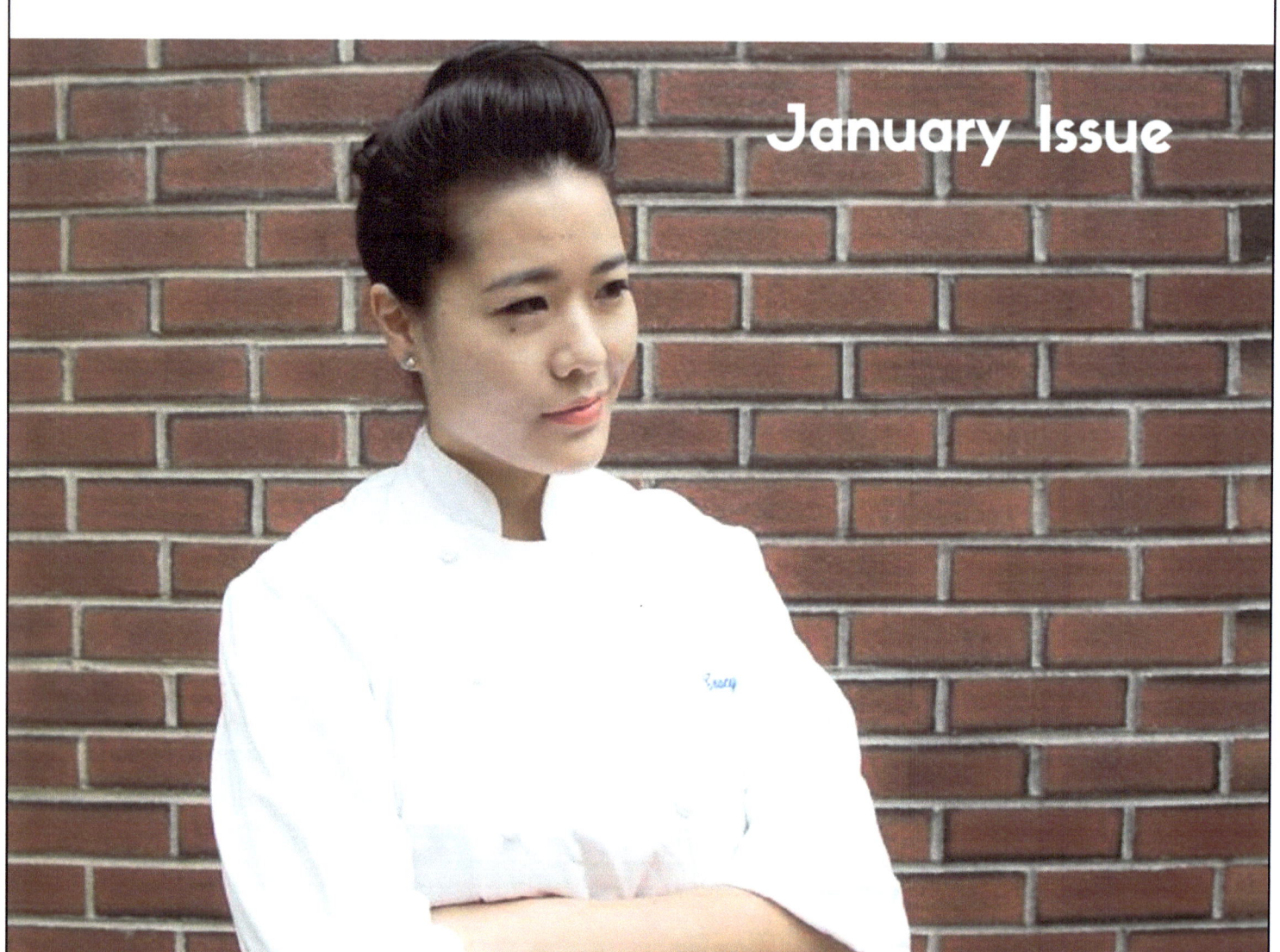

# PAGU

CAMBRIDGE, MA

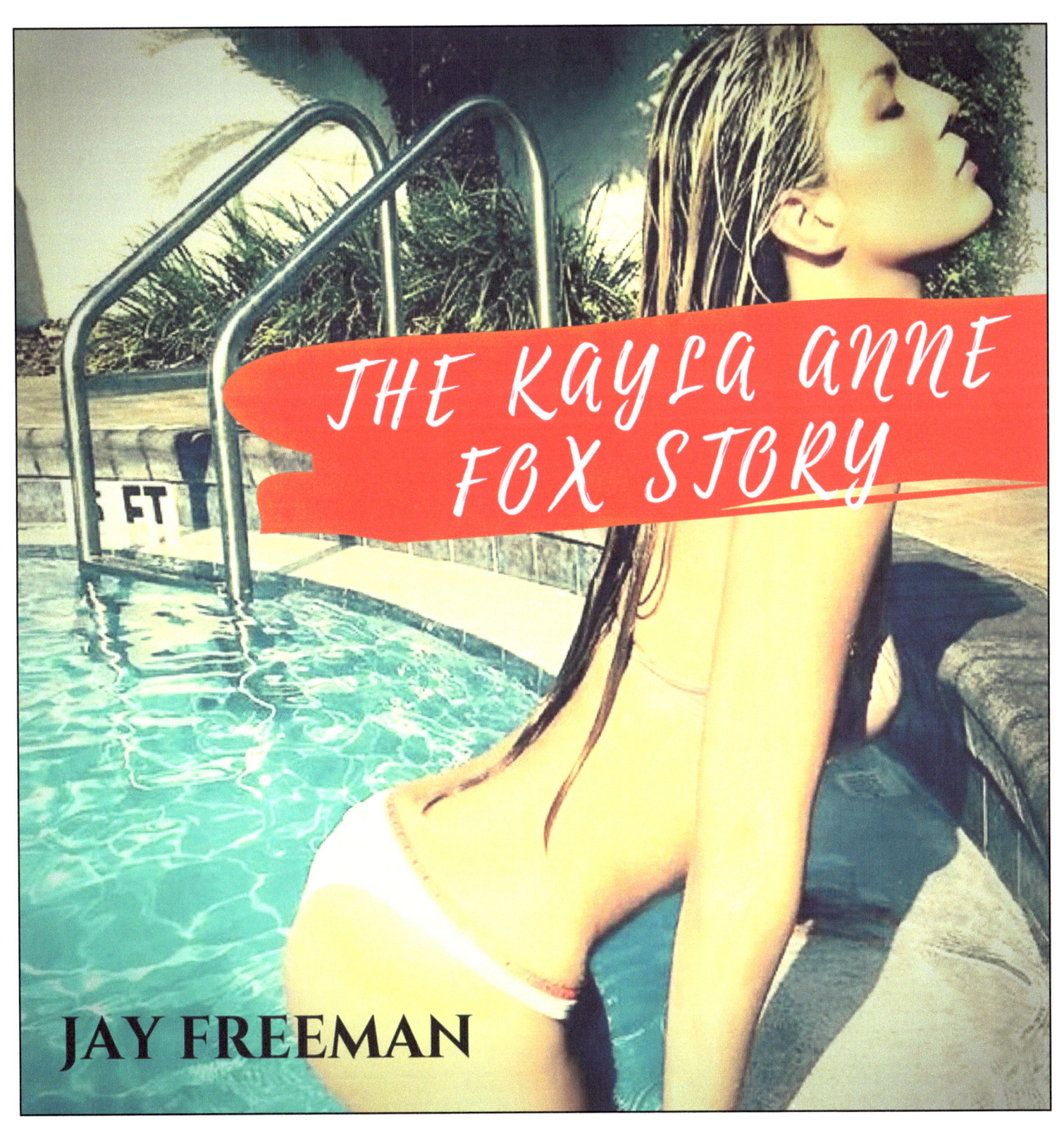

# THE KAYLA ANNE FOX STORY

**JAY FREEMAN**

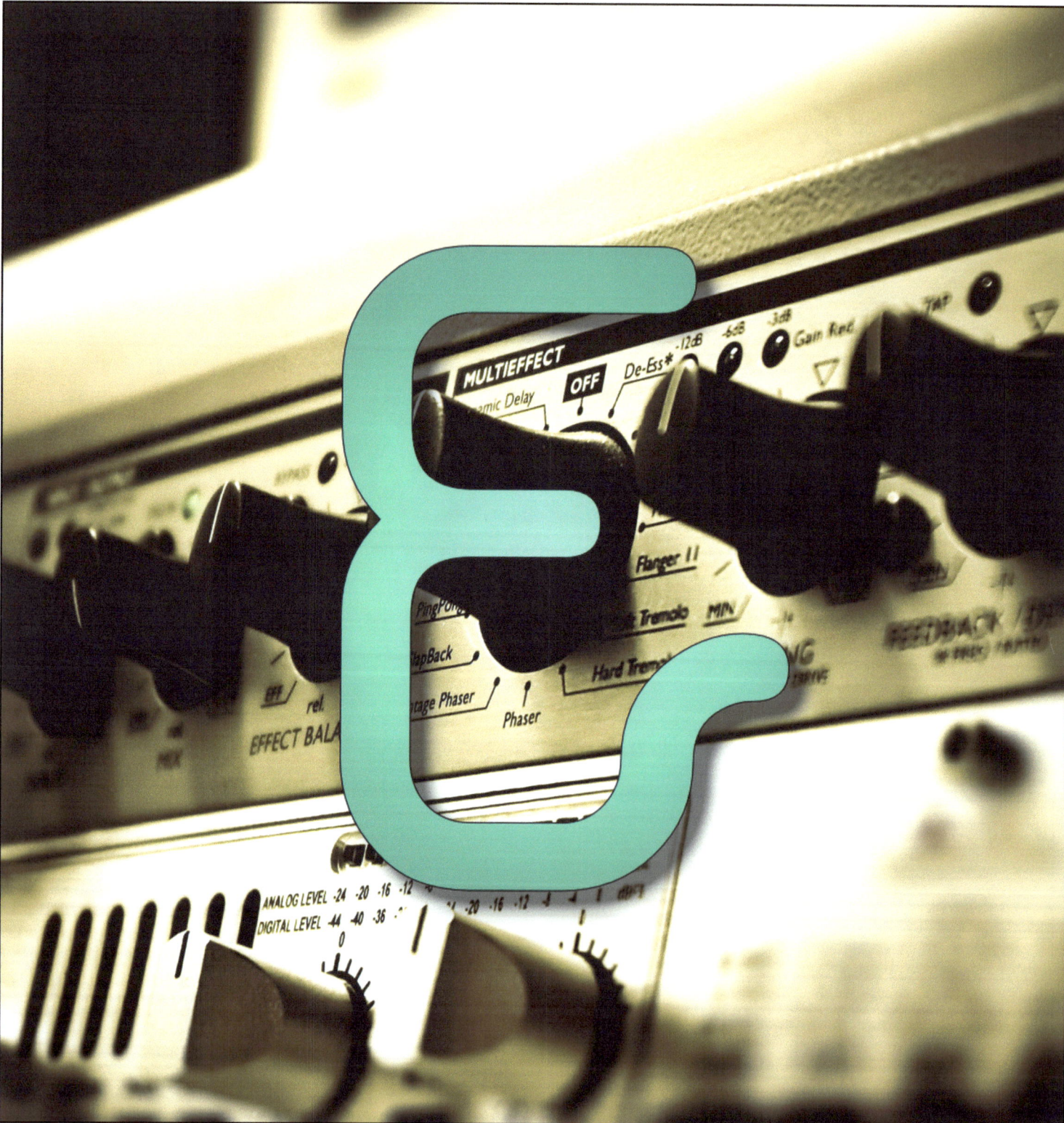

THE
NEW
FACE
IN
MEDIA

BECKLER PUBLISHING

THE NAKED TRUTH MAGAZINE

TRUTH

AMERICA'S VOICE UNFILTERED

JANUARY 2017 | ISSUE NO 6

naked truth magazine

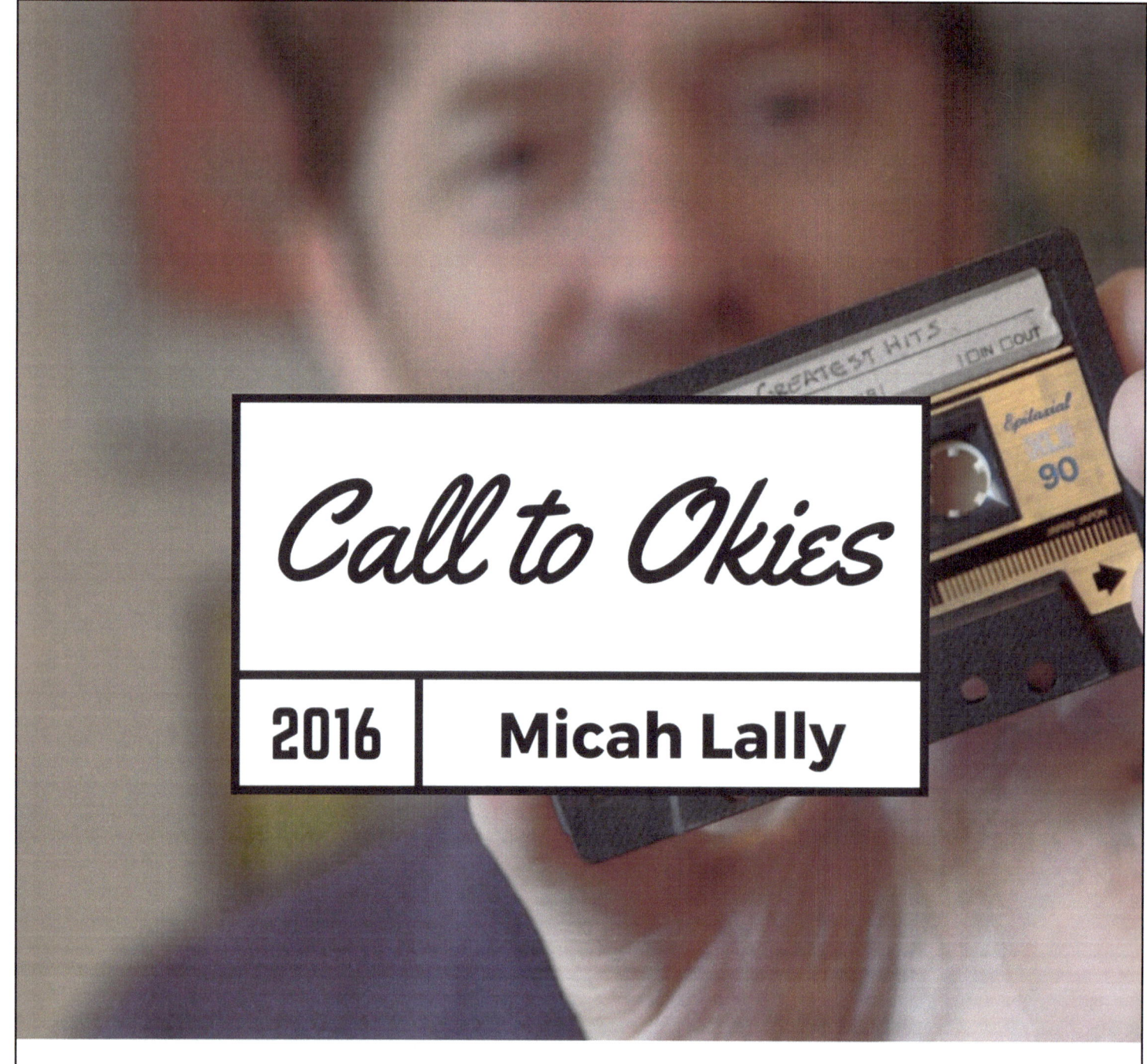

# Call to Okies

| 2016 | Micah Lally |

# A FILM REVIEW BY MICAH LALLY

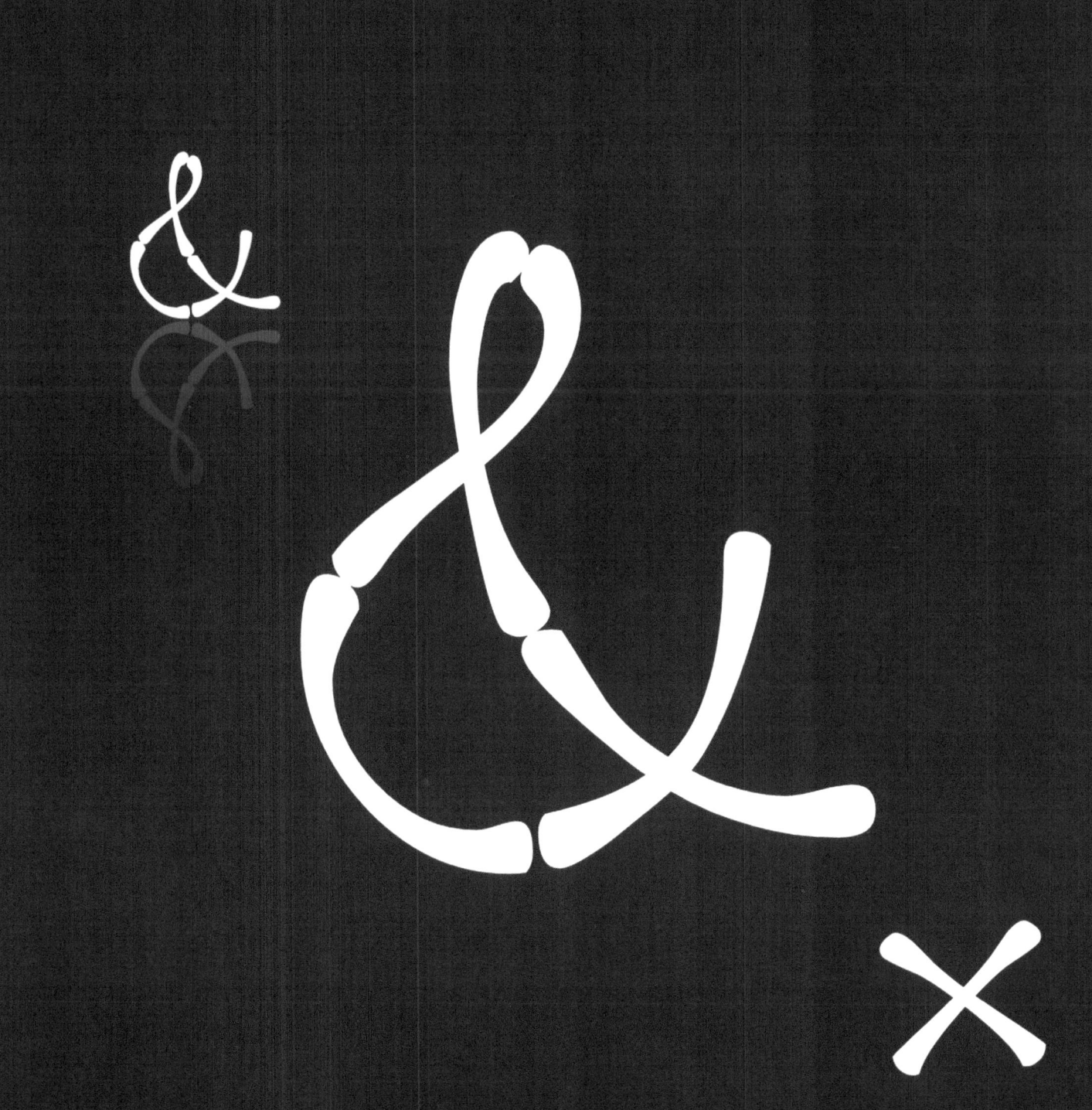

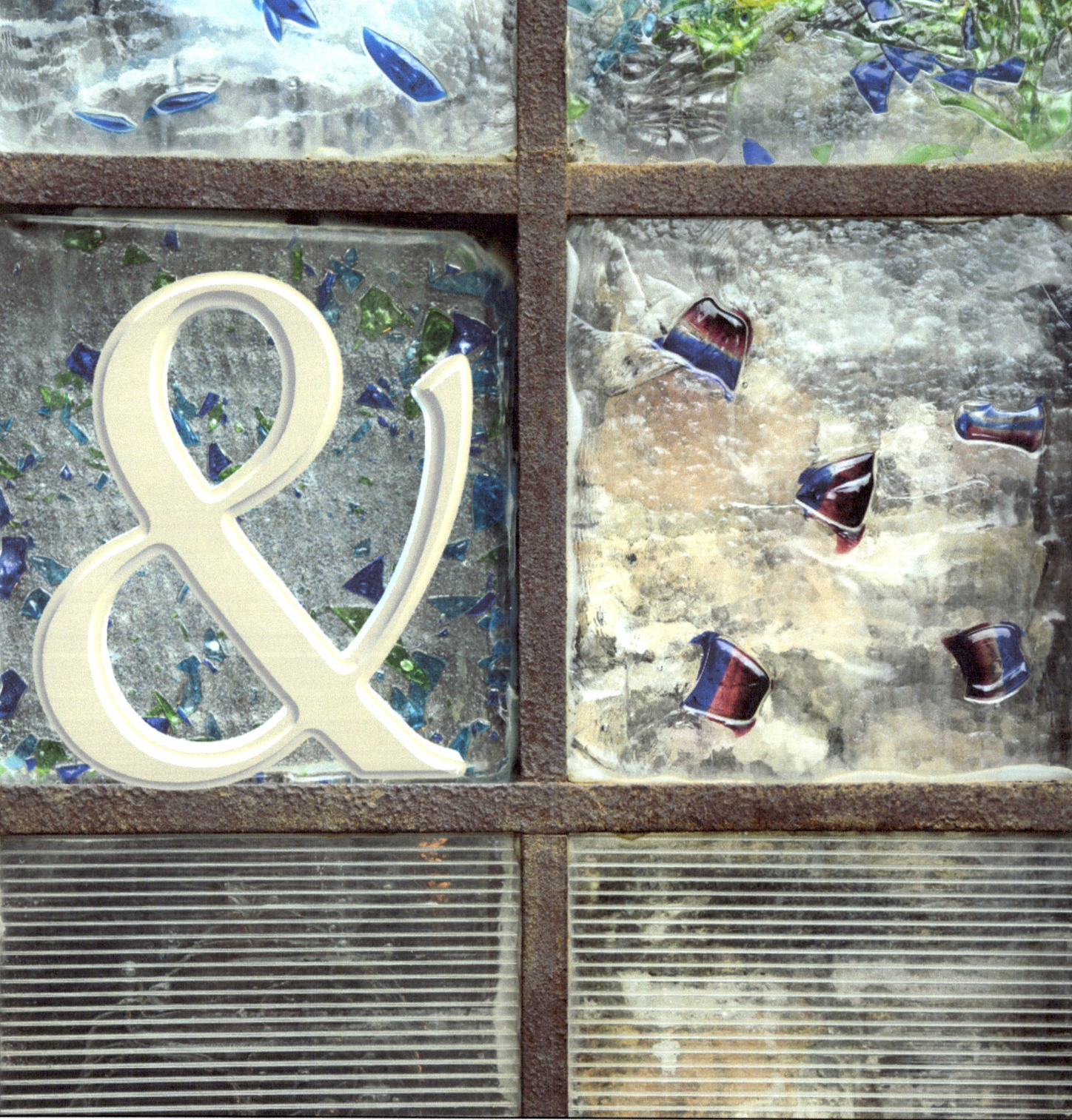

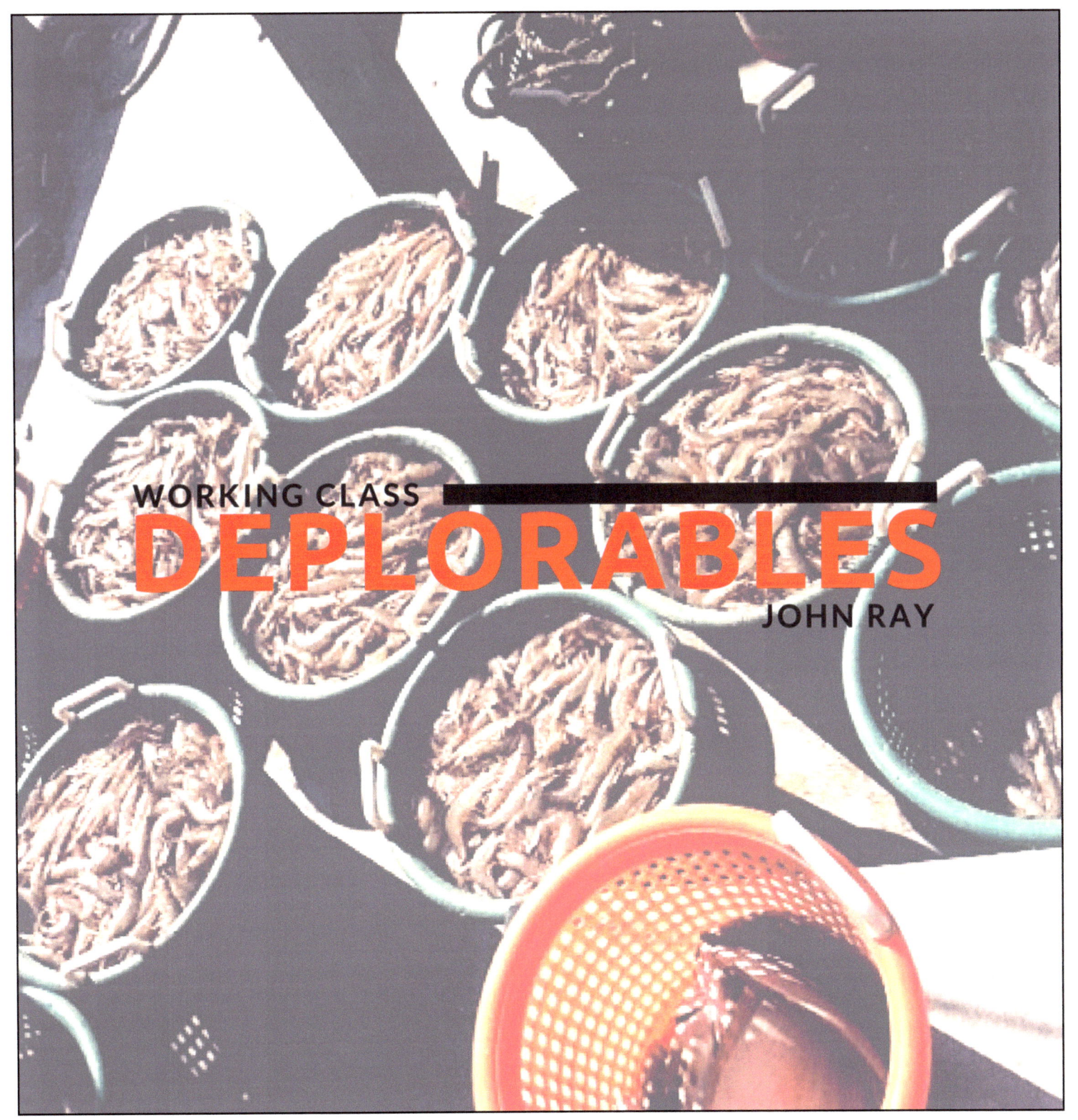

WORKING CLASS
# DEPLORABLES
JOHN RAY

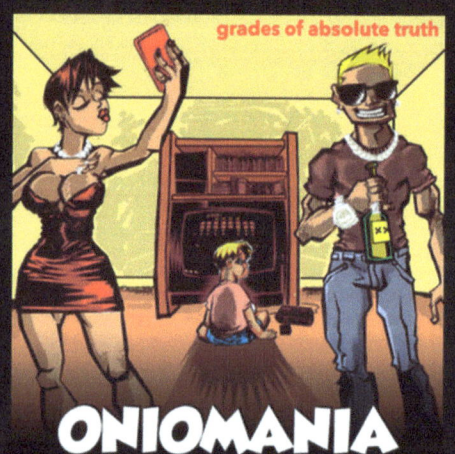

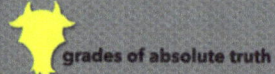

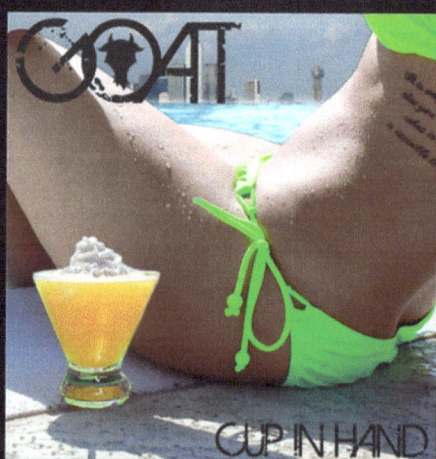

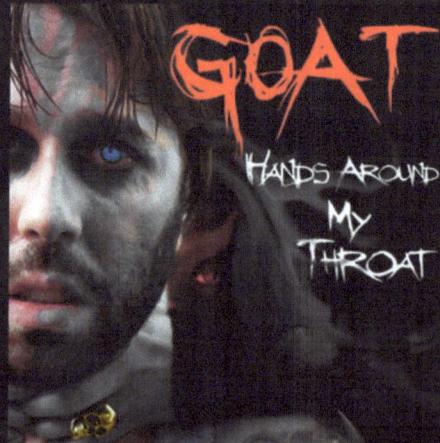

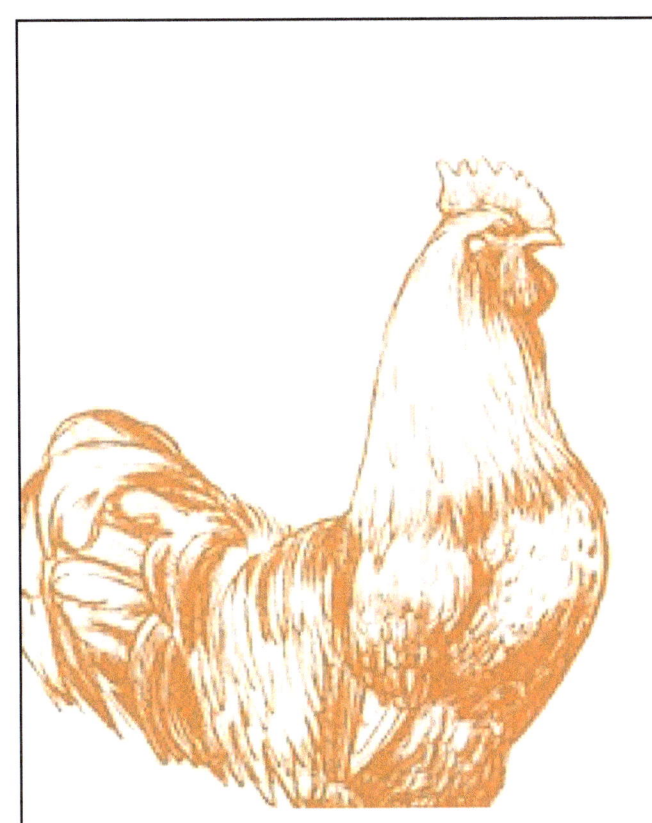

# Matt's MEALS

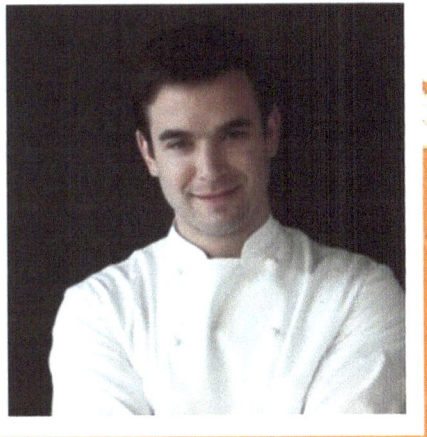

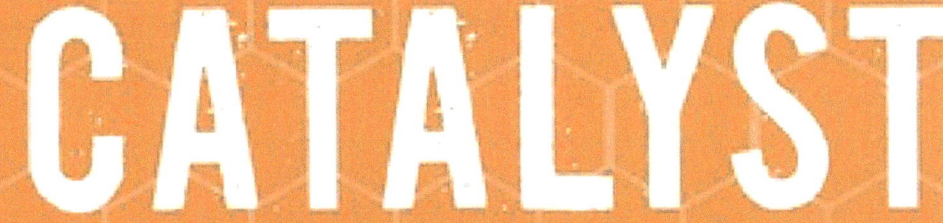

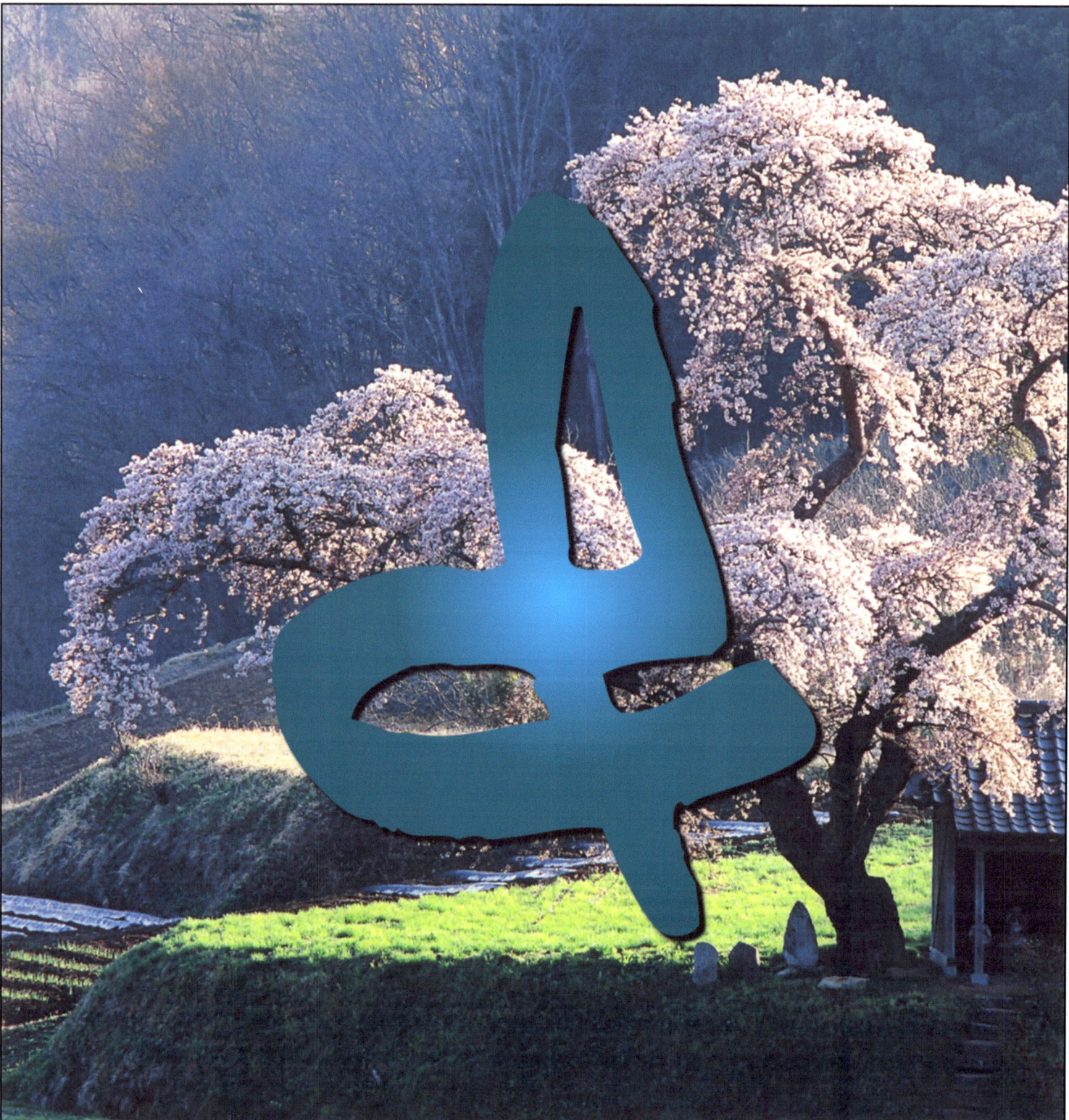

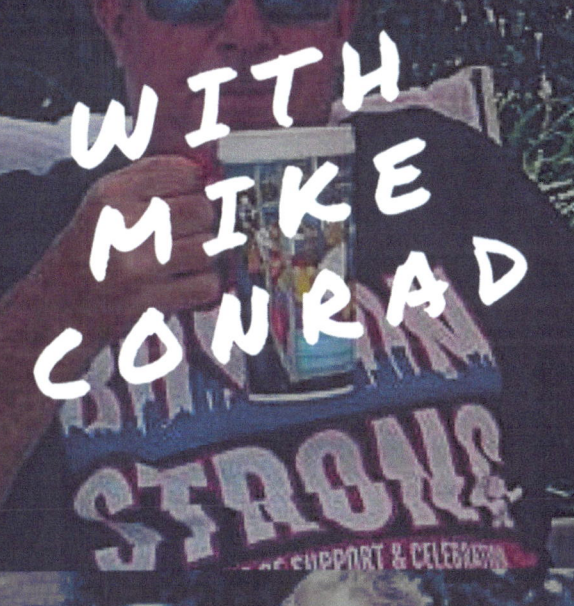

WITH MIKE CONRAD

GOTTA HAVE
GADGET

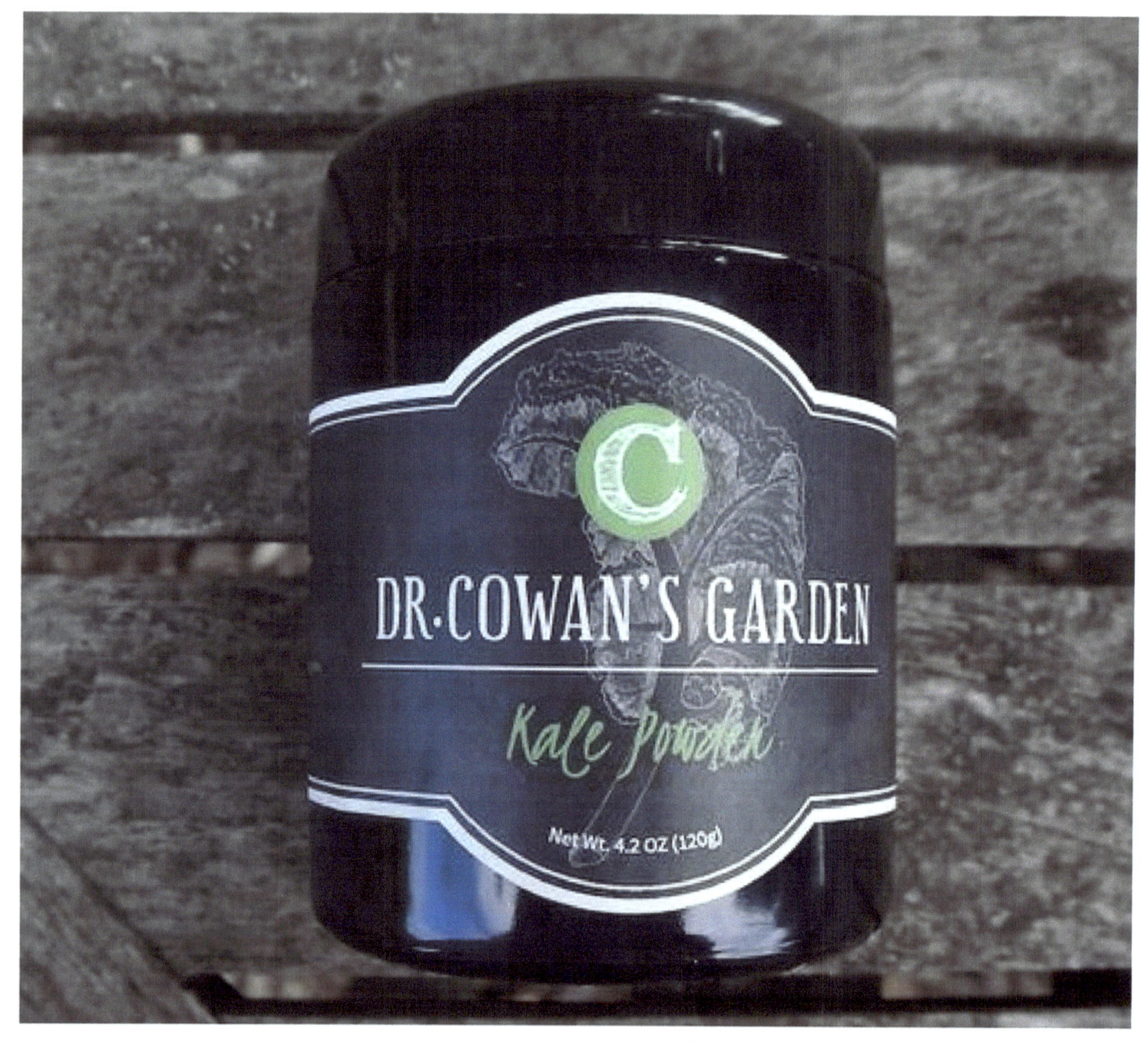

MATT ROBINSON'S BLOWING UP

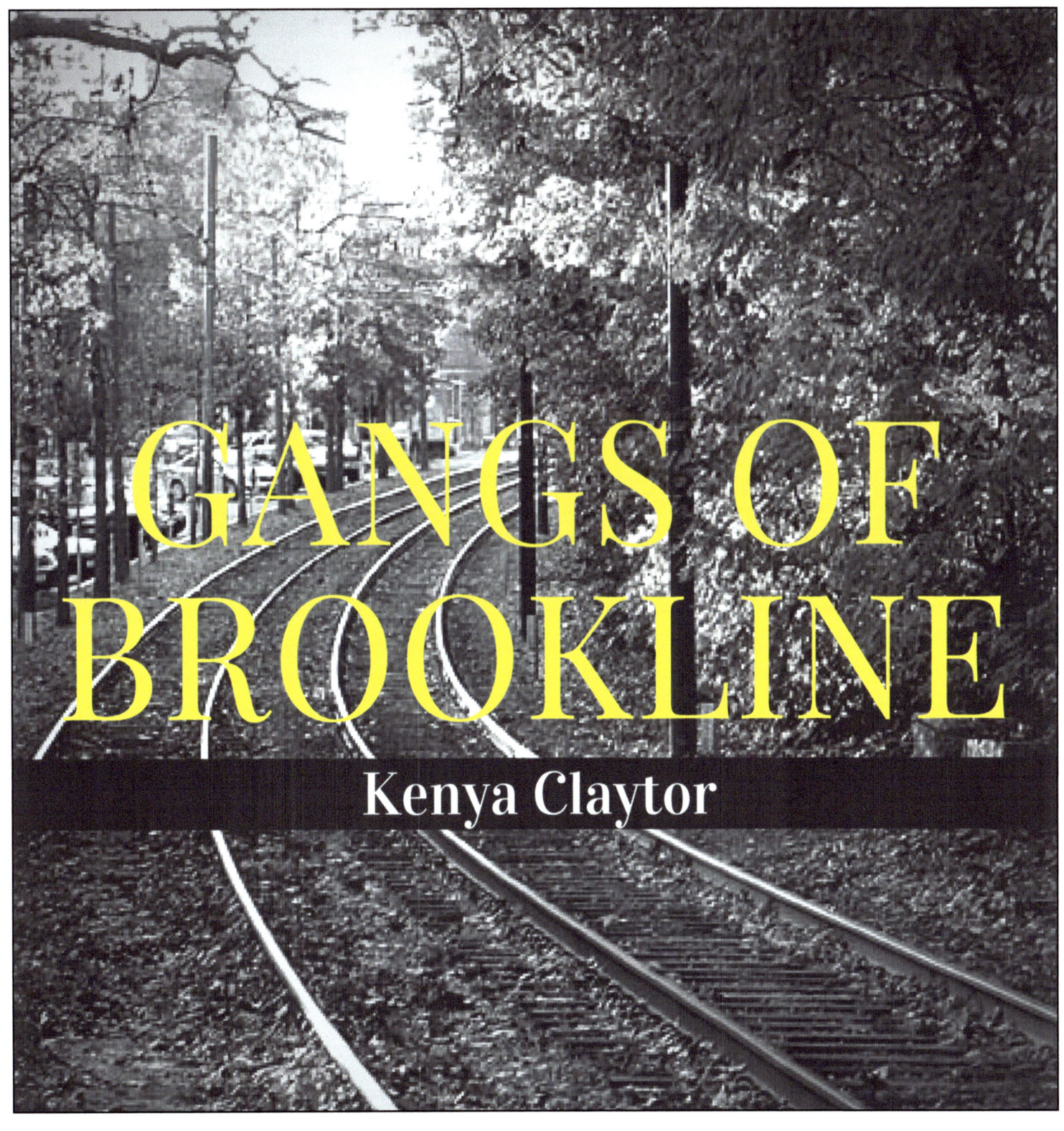

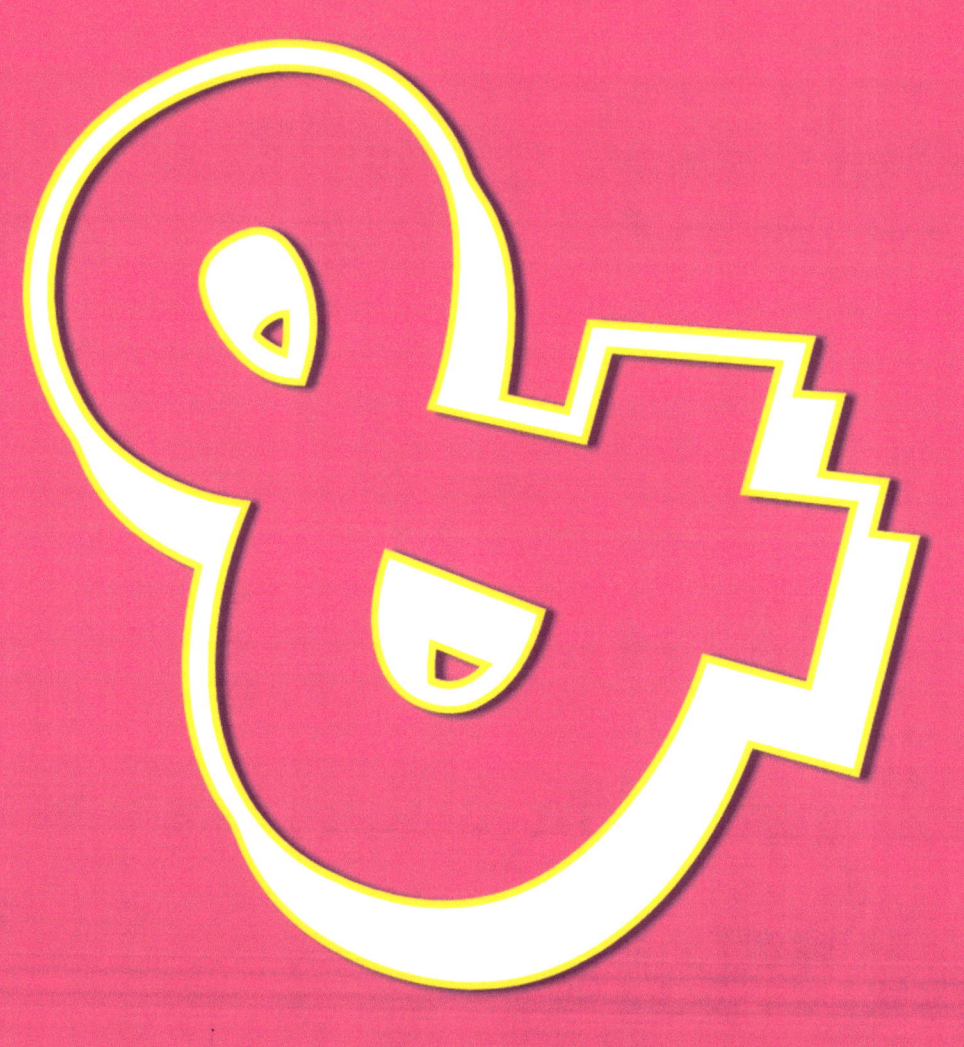

# KINKED ABOUT
# DATING

## KERRI M. REHAK

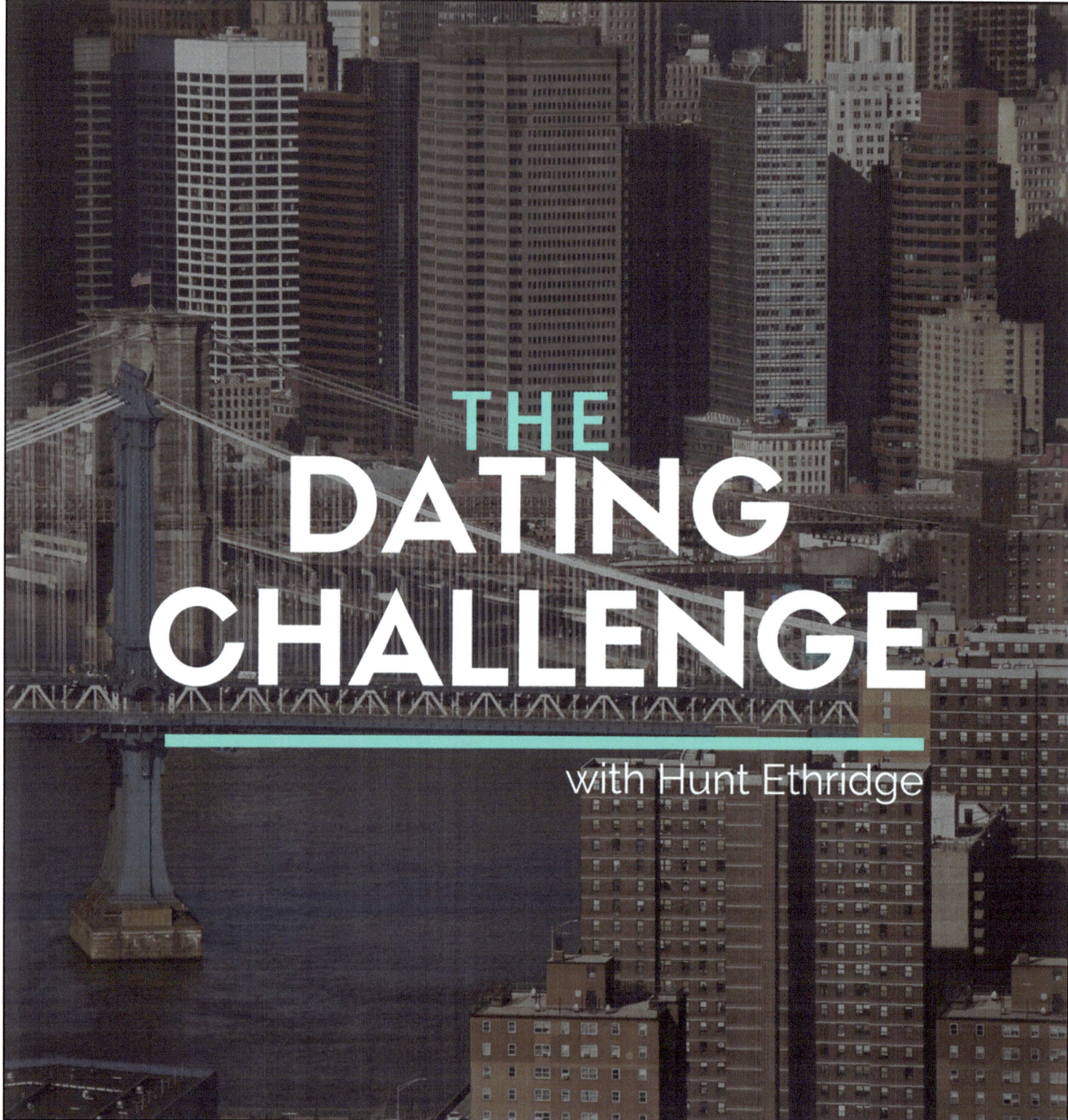

# THE
# DATING
# CHALLENGE

with Hunt Ethridge

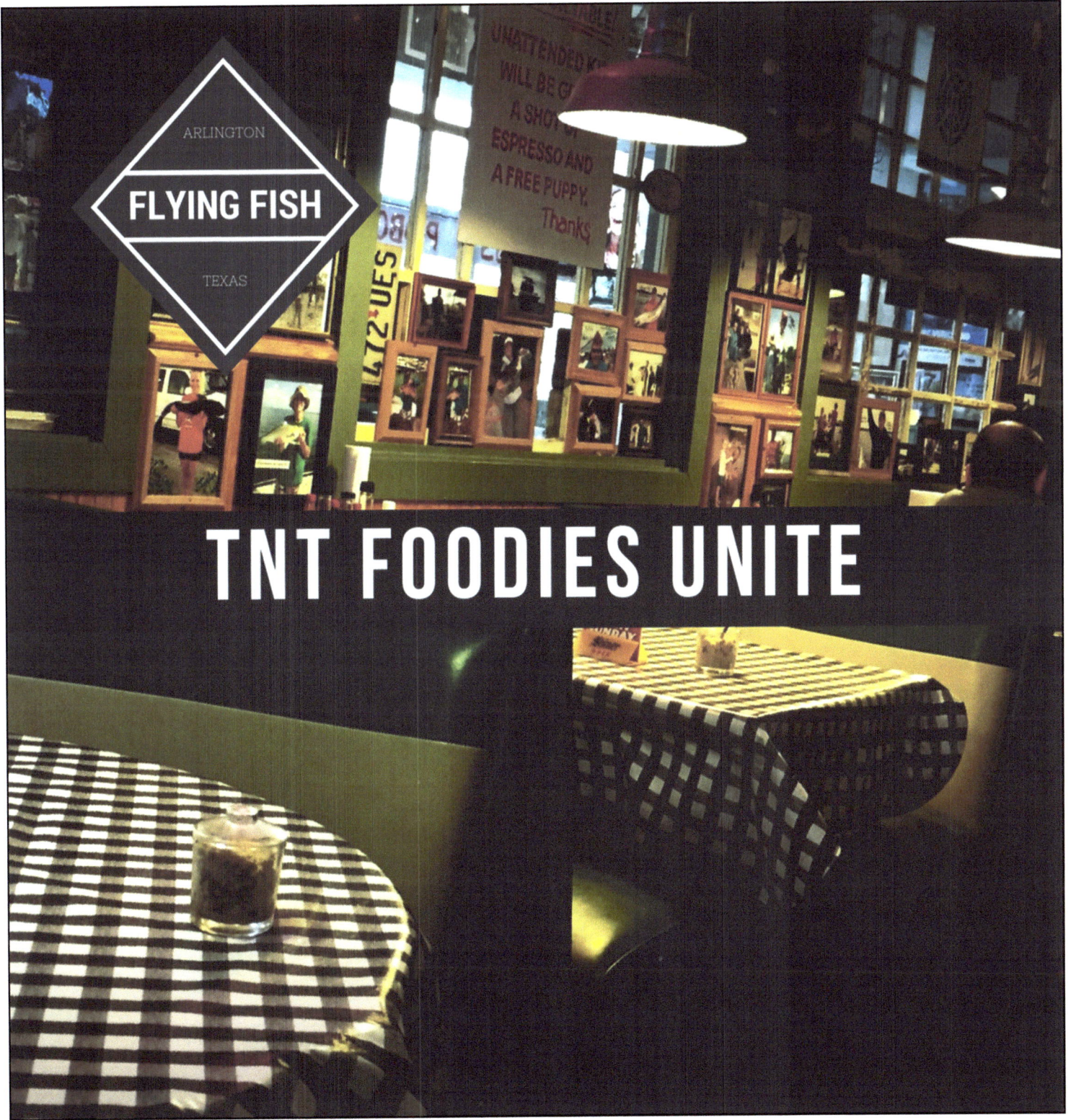

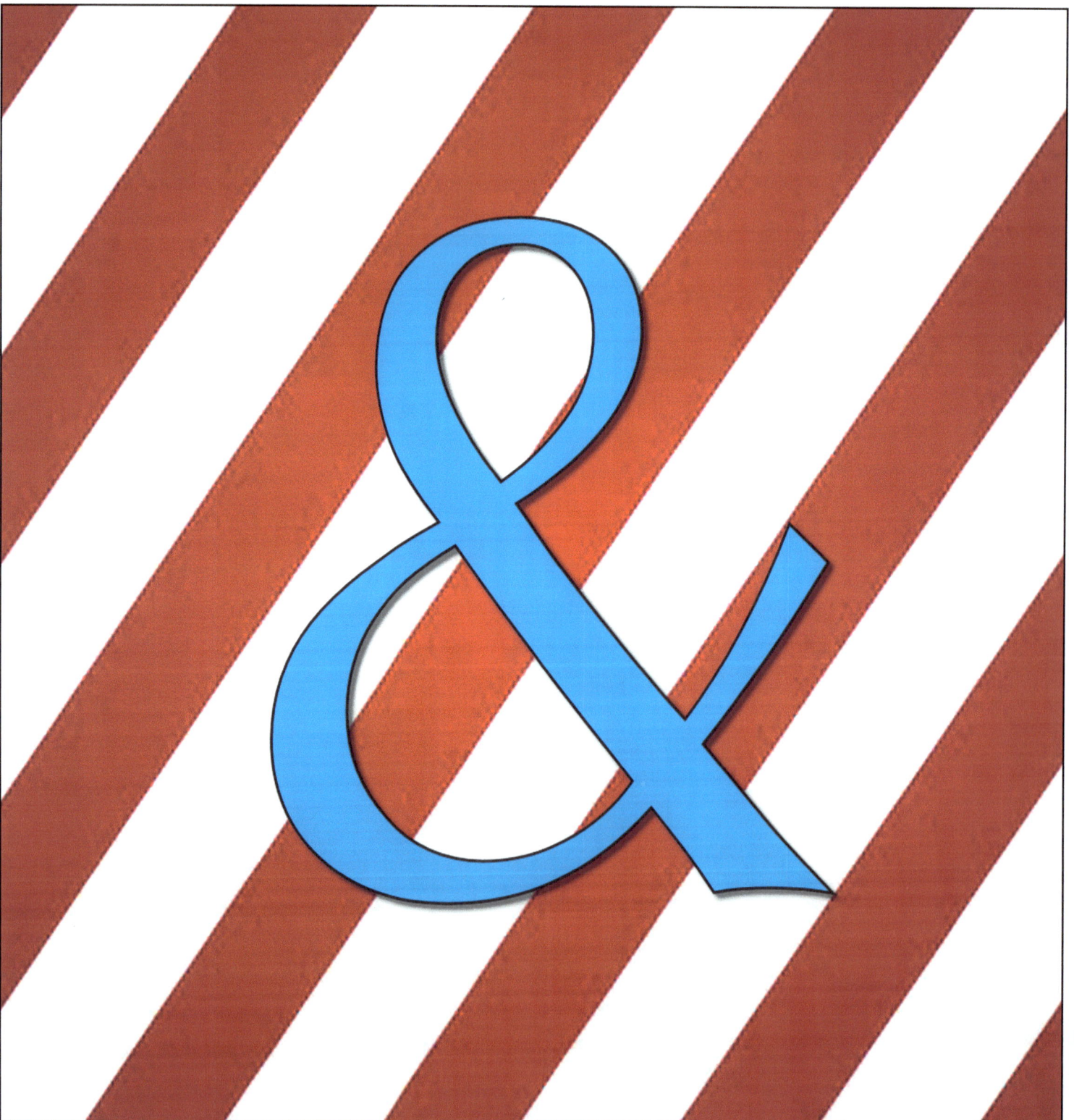

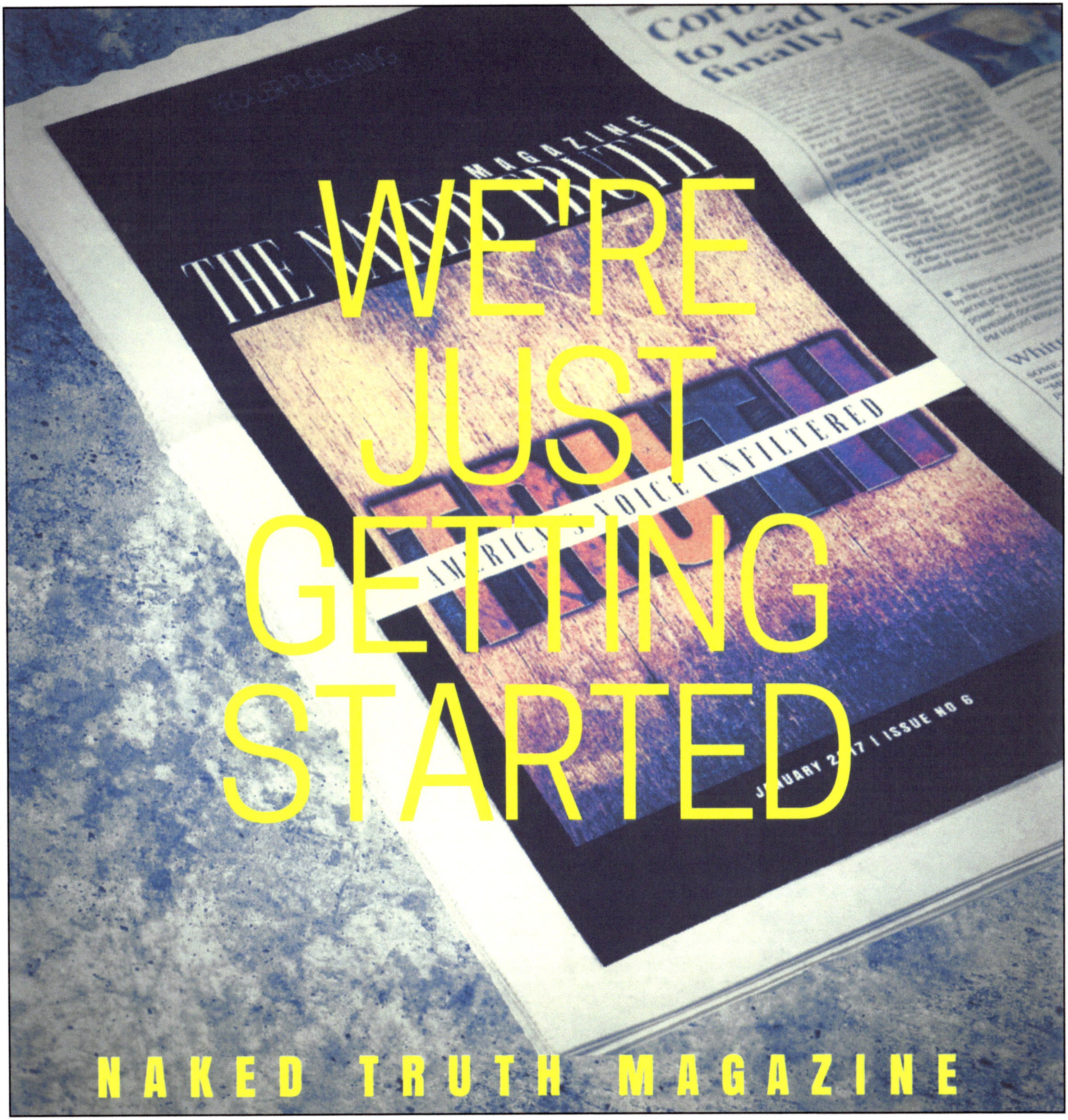

WE'RE JUST GETTING STARTED

NAKED TRUTH MAGAZINE

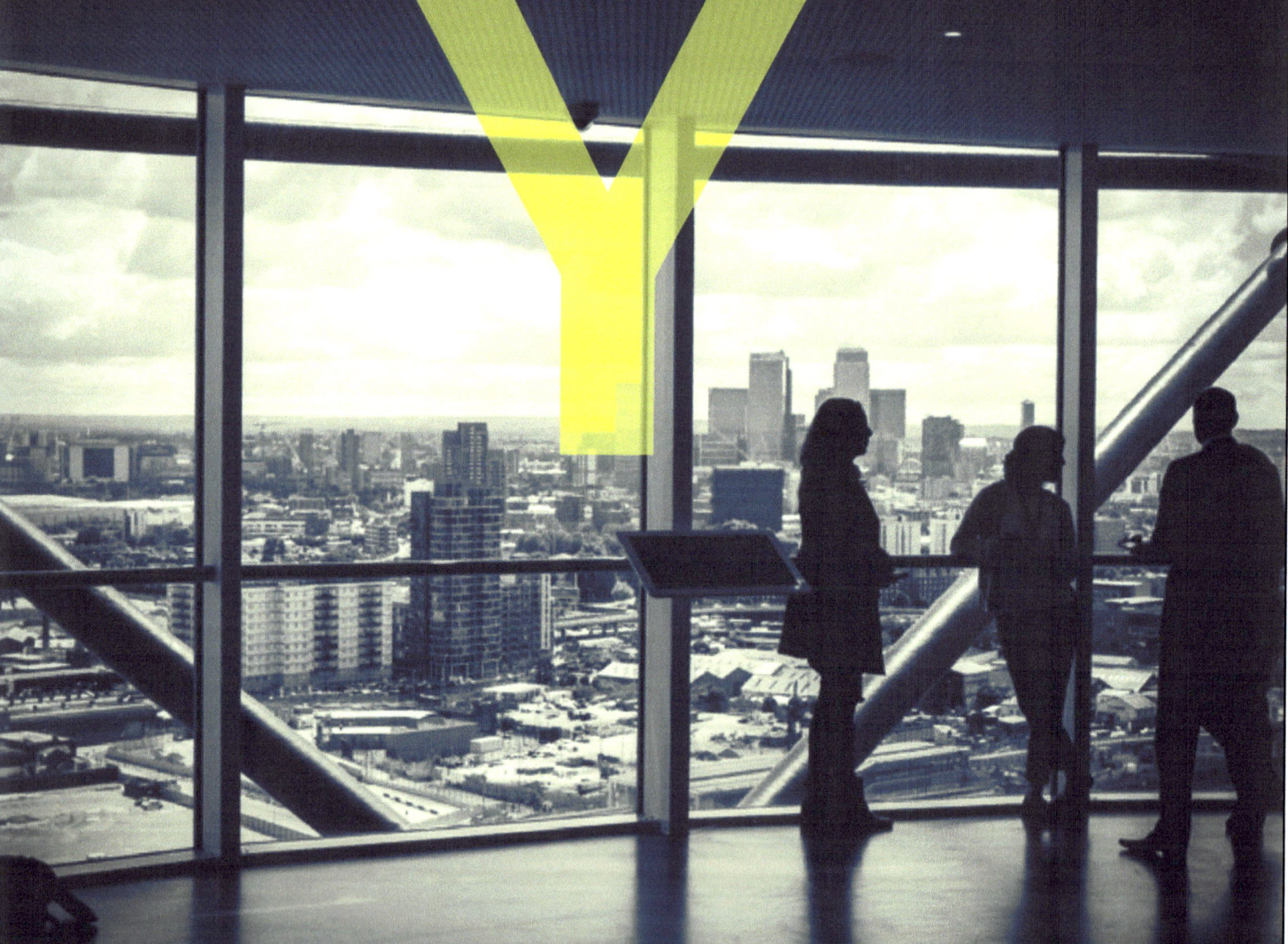

# GENERATION'S

# Y

# A new series by The Naked Truth

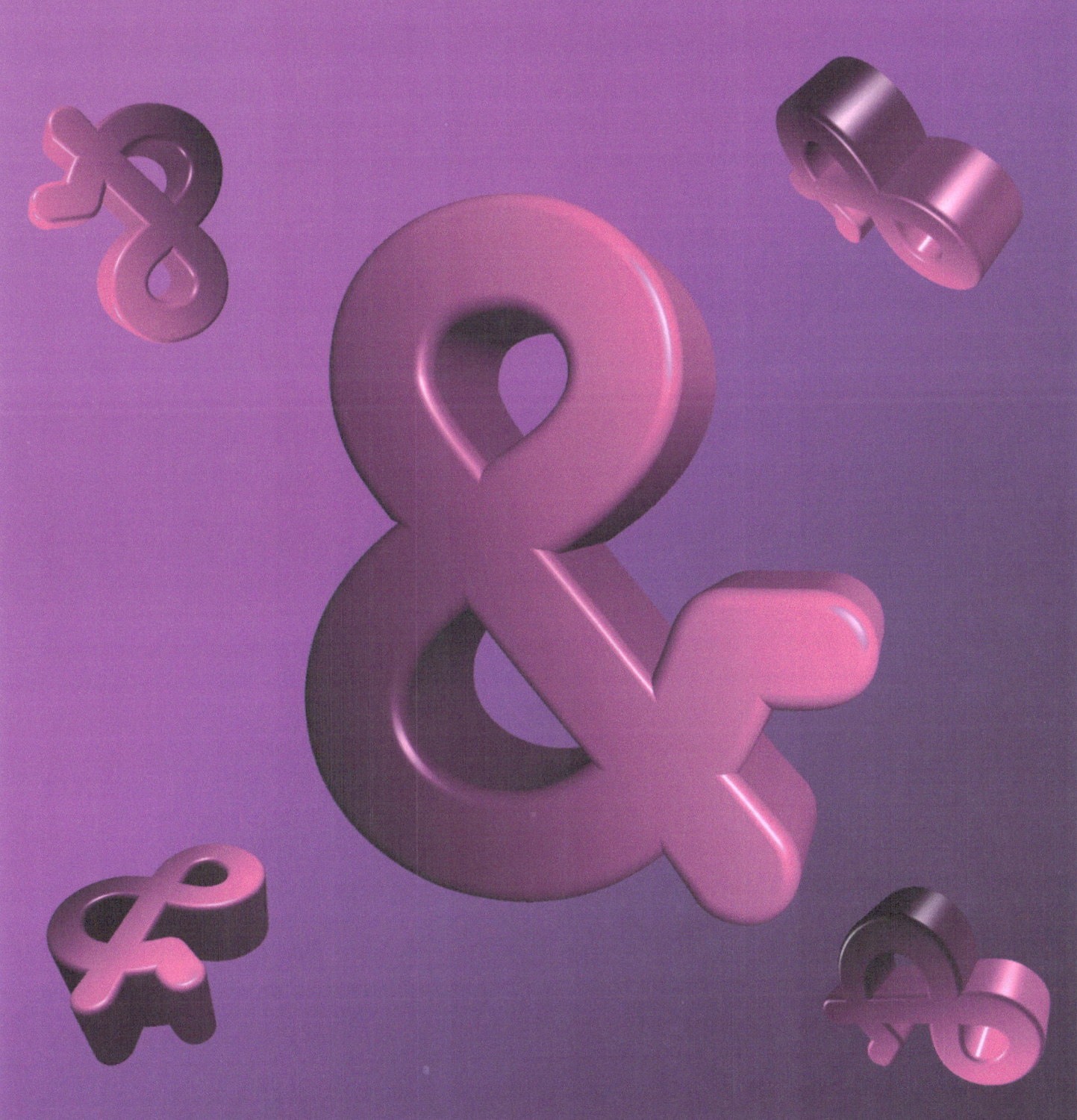

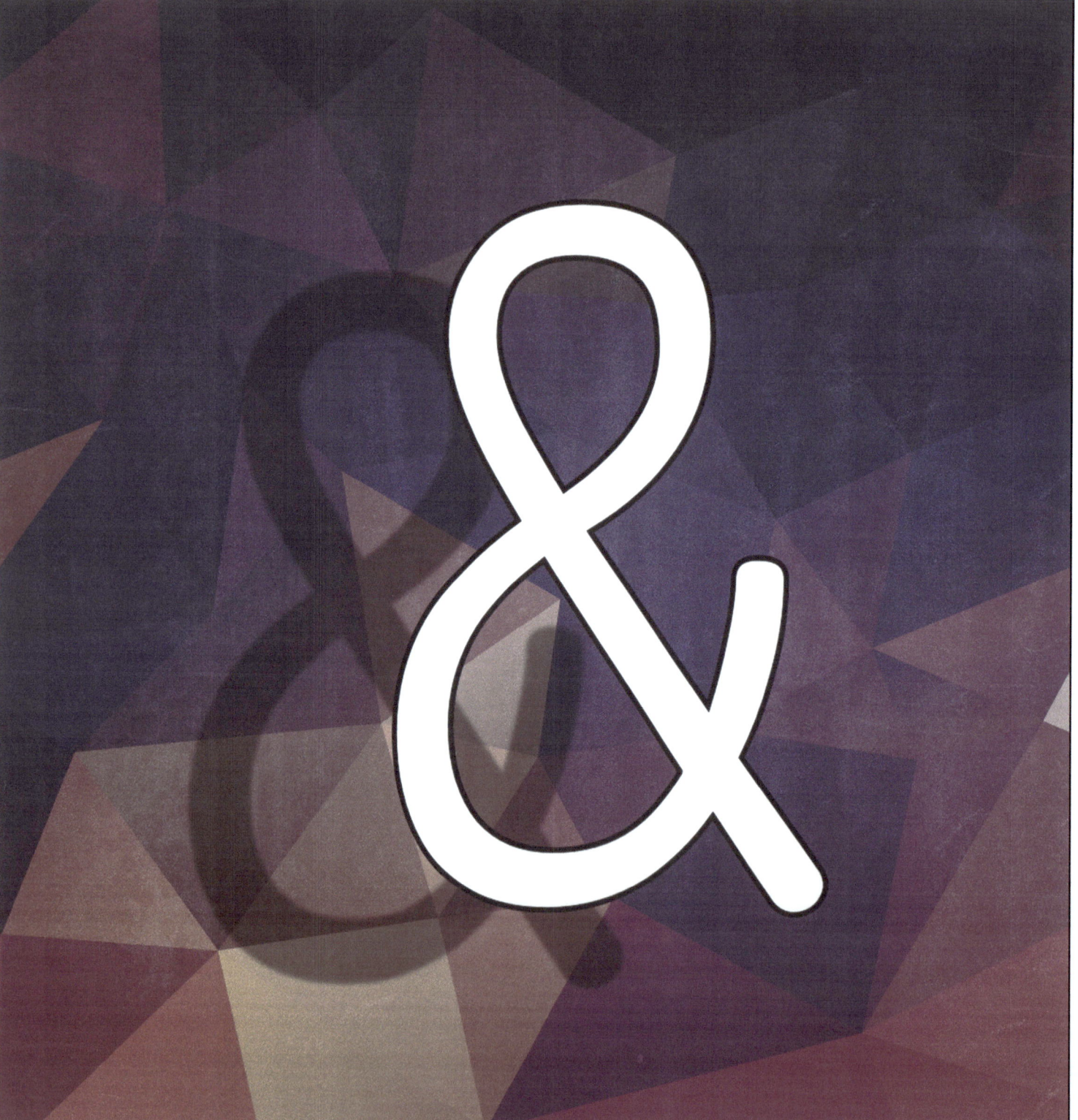

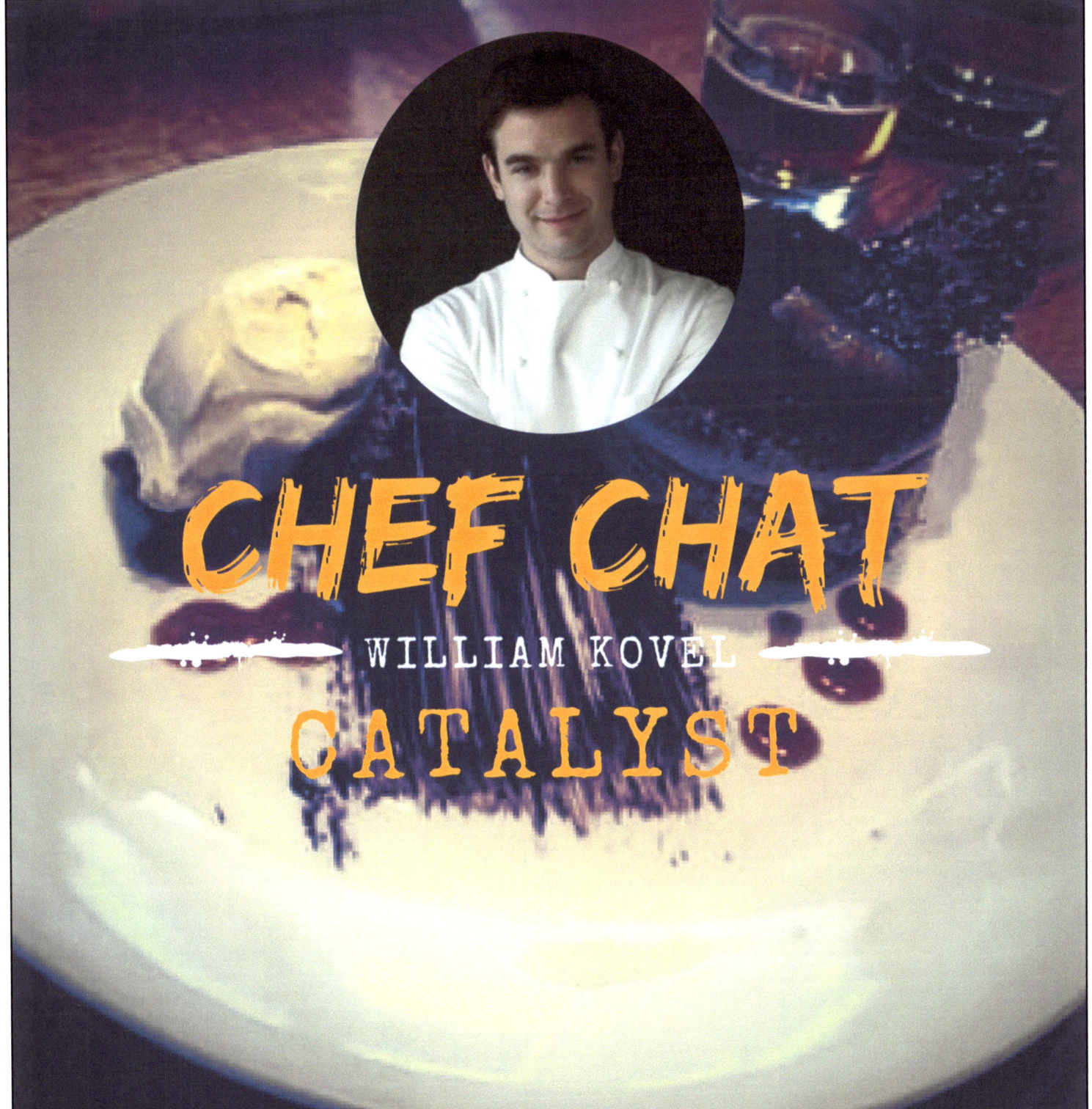

# CHEF CHAT

## WILLIAM KOVEL

### CATALYST

YOUNG ENTREPRENEURS

# MAT RITCHIE

CHANGING THE GAME

# GENERATION'S

## A new series by The Naked Truth

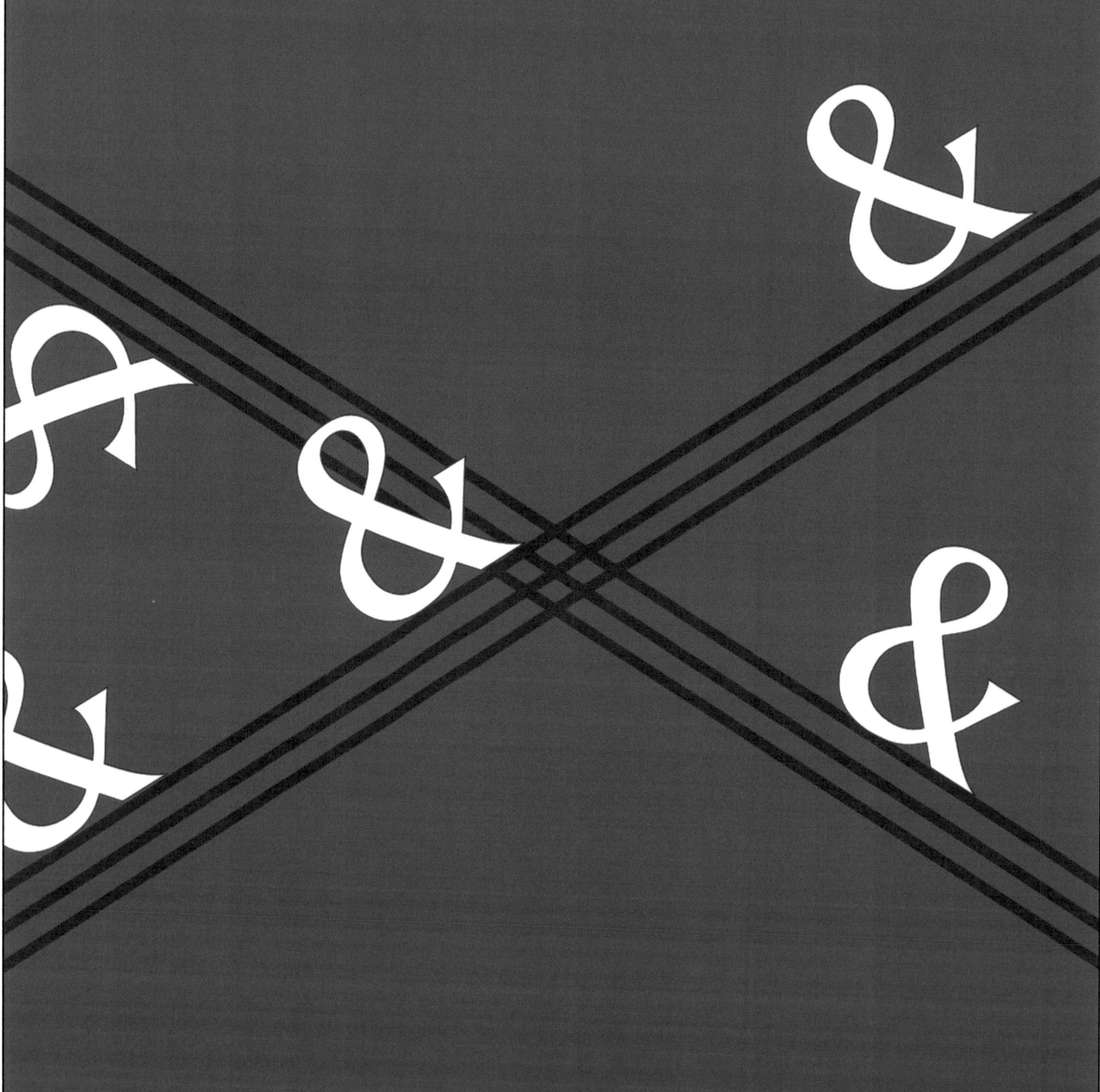

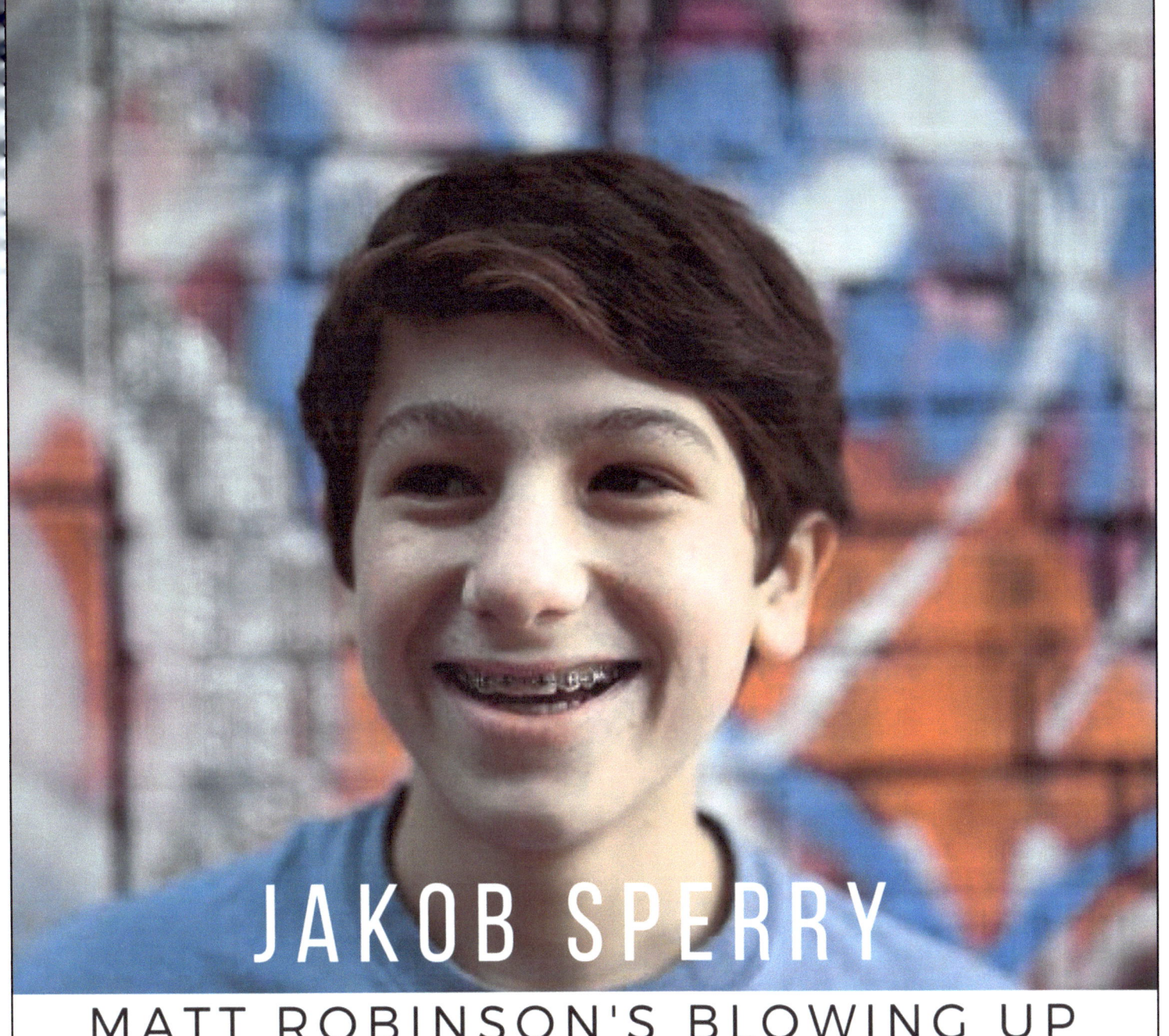

# JAKOB SPERRY
## MATT ROBINSON'S BLOWING UP

# the
# Producer's Desk

## Guest Spotlight

# MICHAEL HEATHEN

EDITOR'S BIRTHDAY MONTH GIVEAWAY

NOW UNTIL MARCH 1ST

FREE ANNUAL SUBSCRIPTION

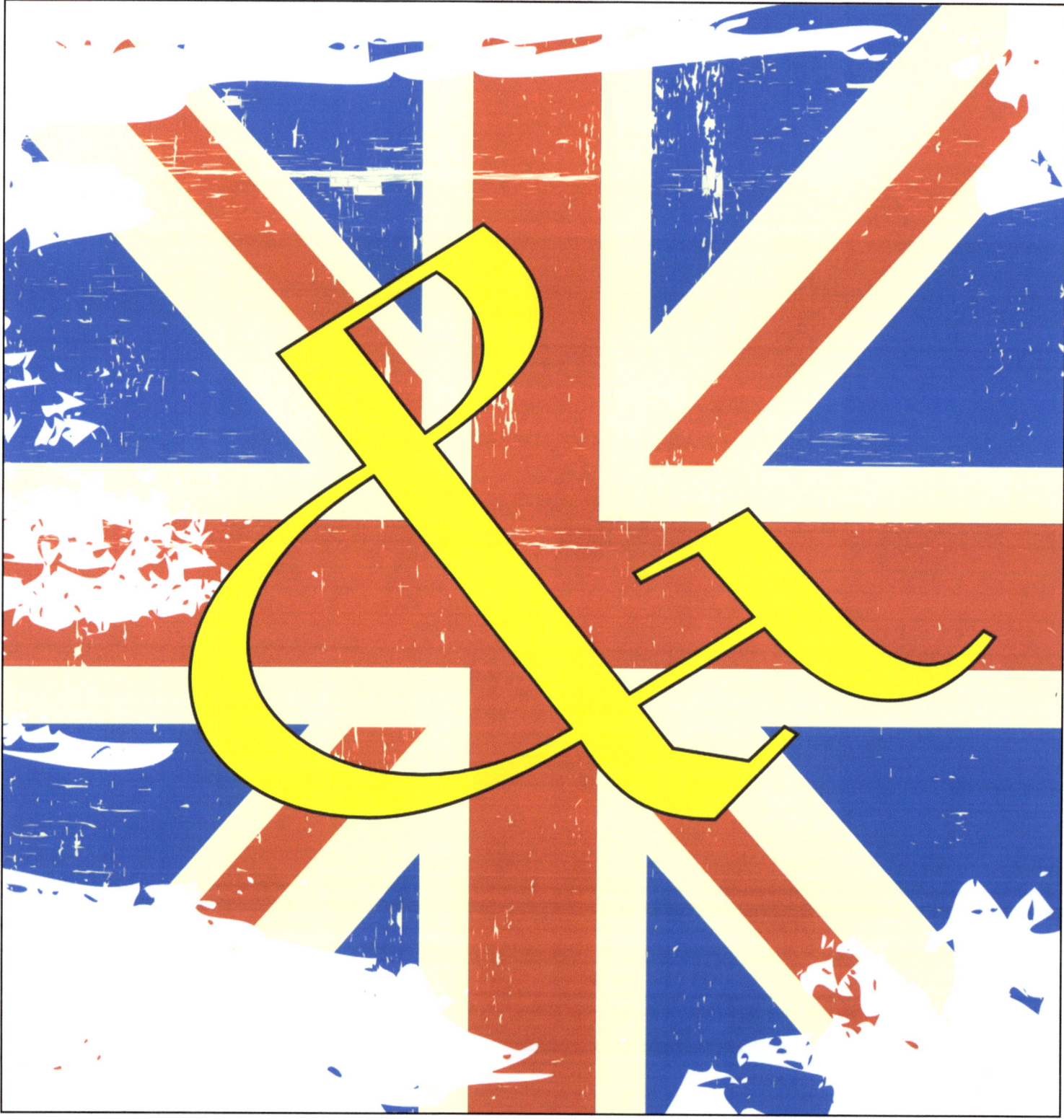

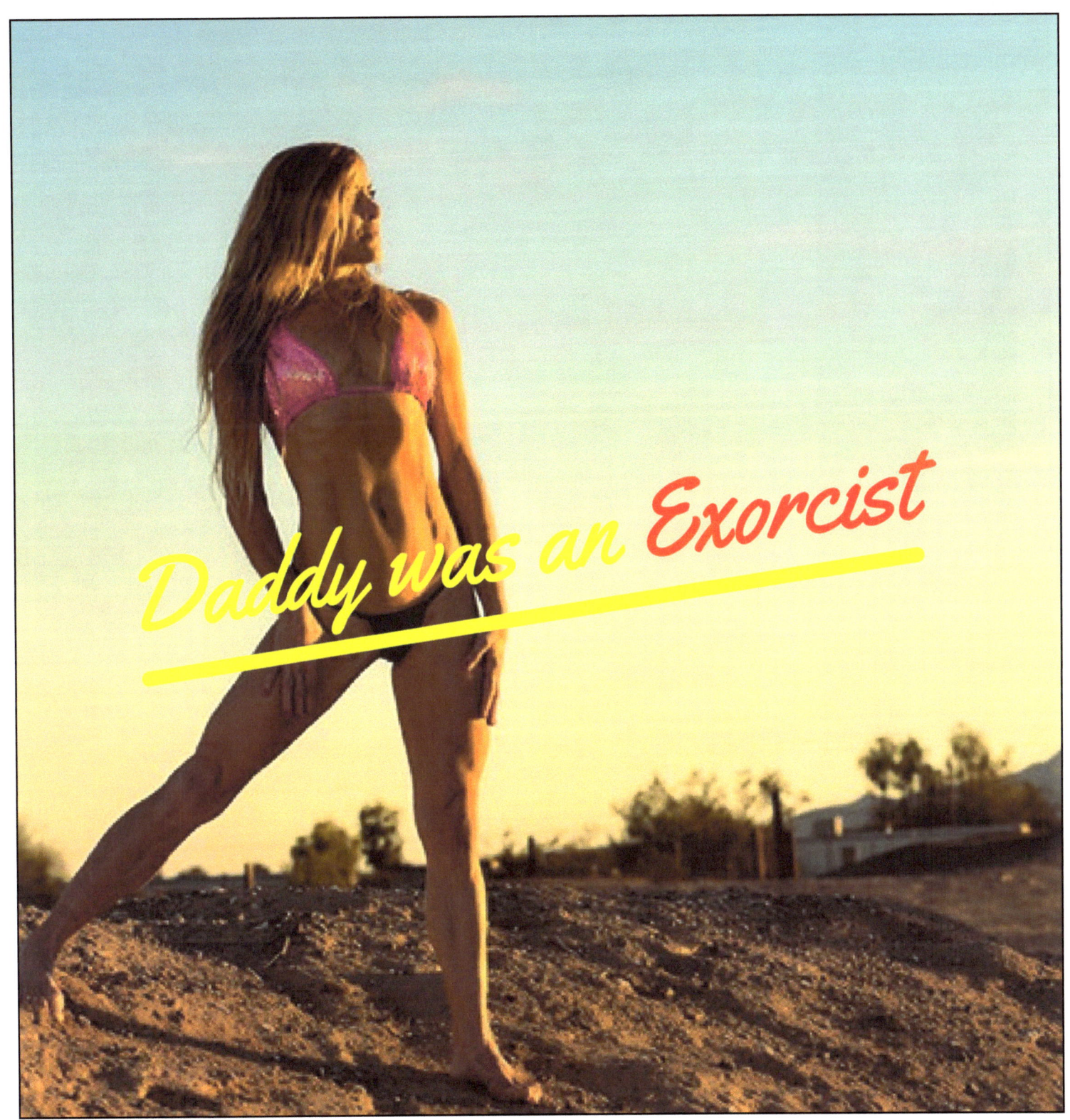

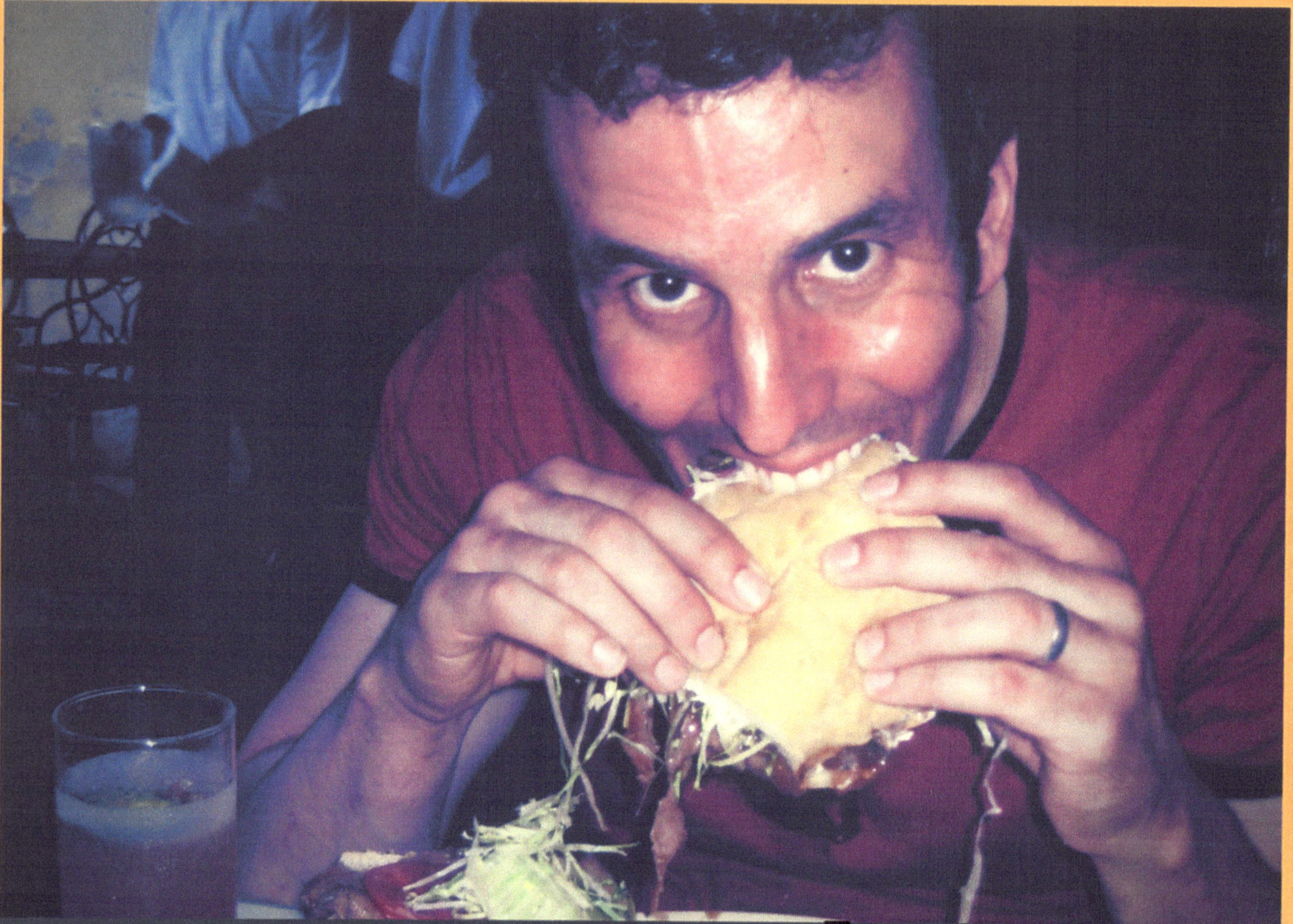

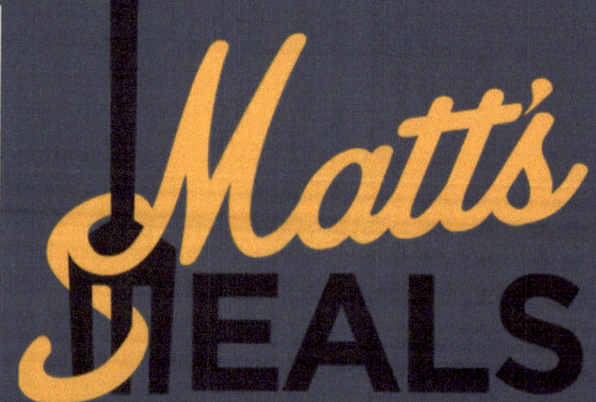

NAKED TRUTH MAGAZINE

MATT ROBINSON
TEARING UP THE NEW
ENGLAND FOOD SCENE ONE
MEAL AT A TIME.

*Matt's* MEALS

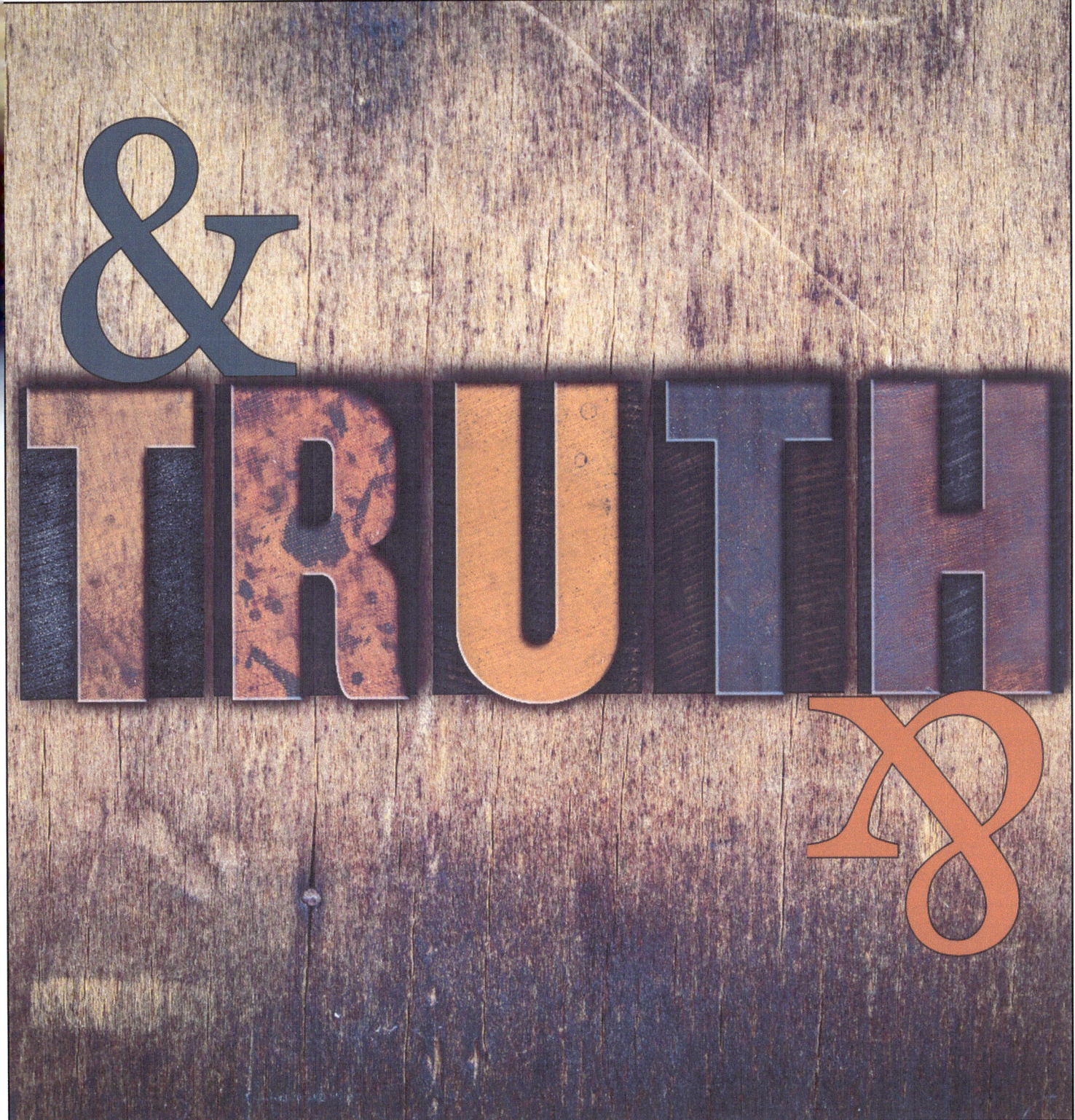

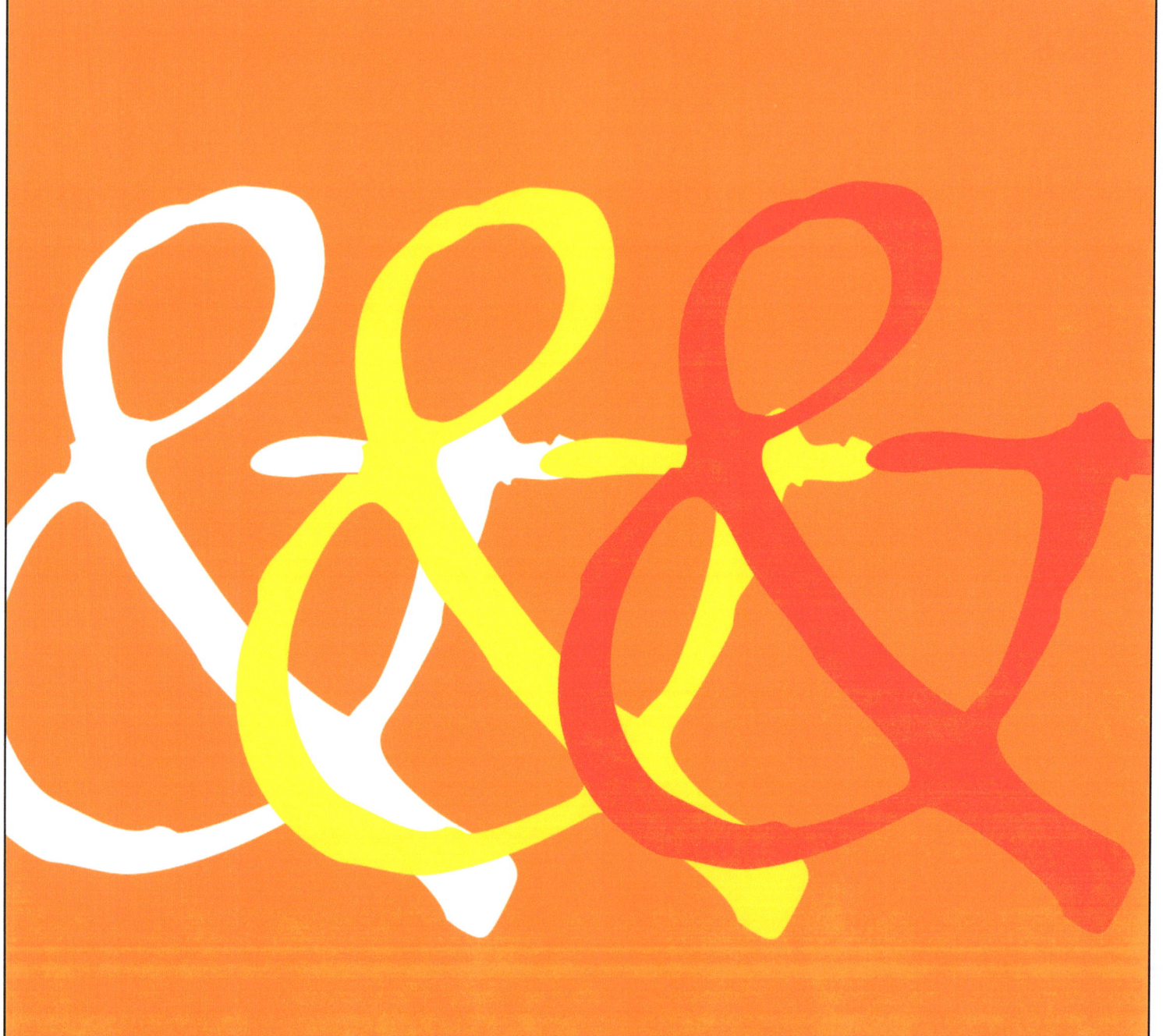

ON
OUR
WAY
UP

BECHLER PUBLISHING

# THE NAKED TRUTH

MAGAZINE

**TRUTH**

AMERICA'S VOICE UNFILTERED

JANUARY 2017 | ISSUE NO 6

JANUARY ISSUE

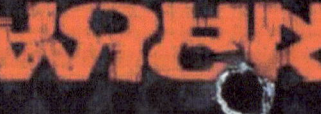

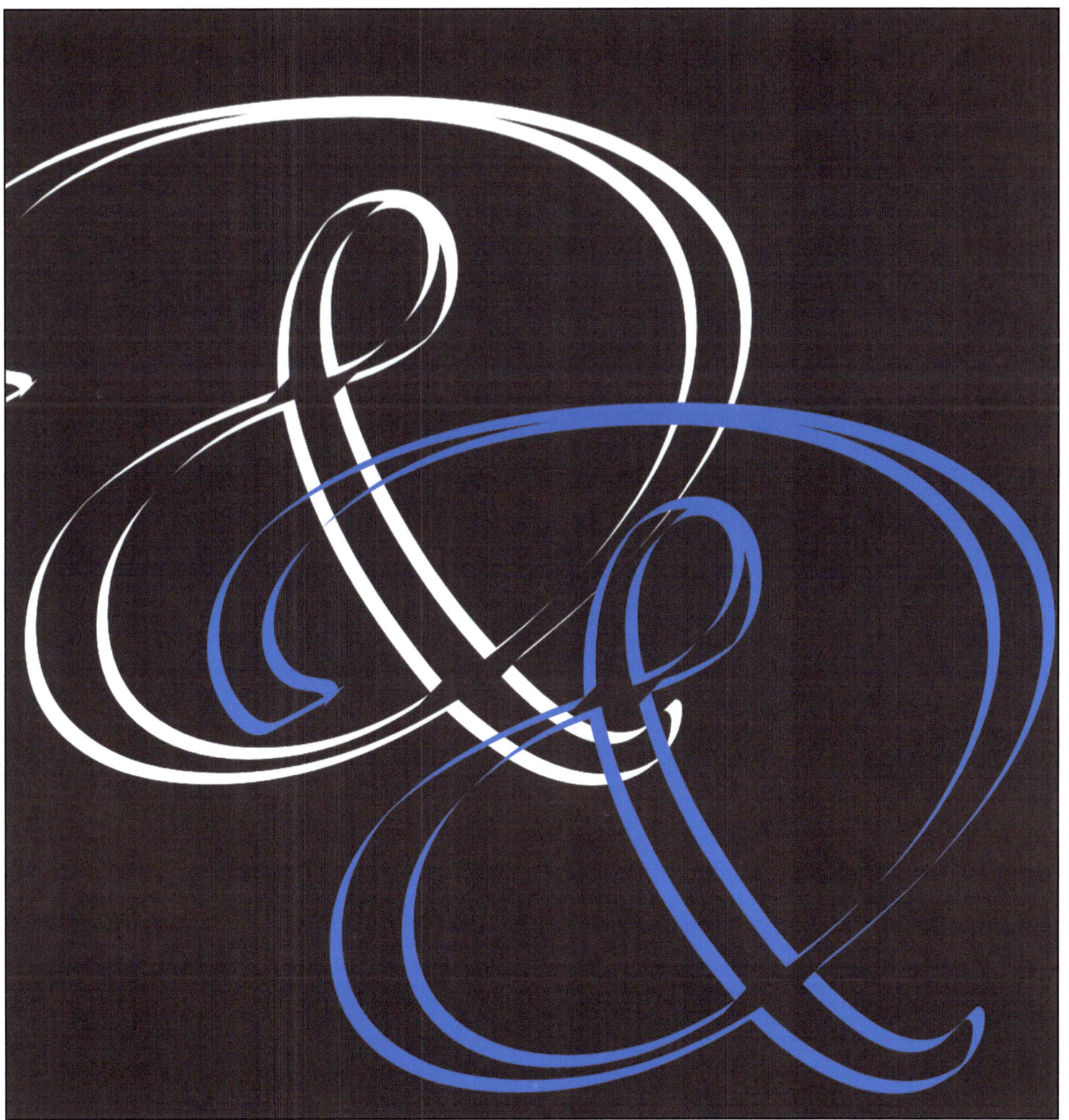

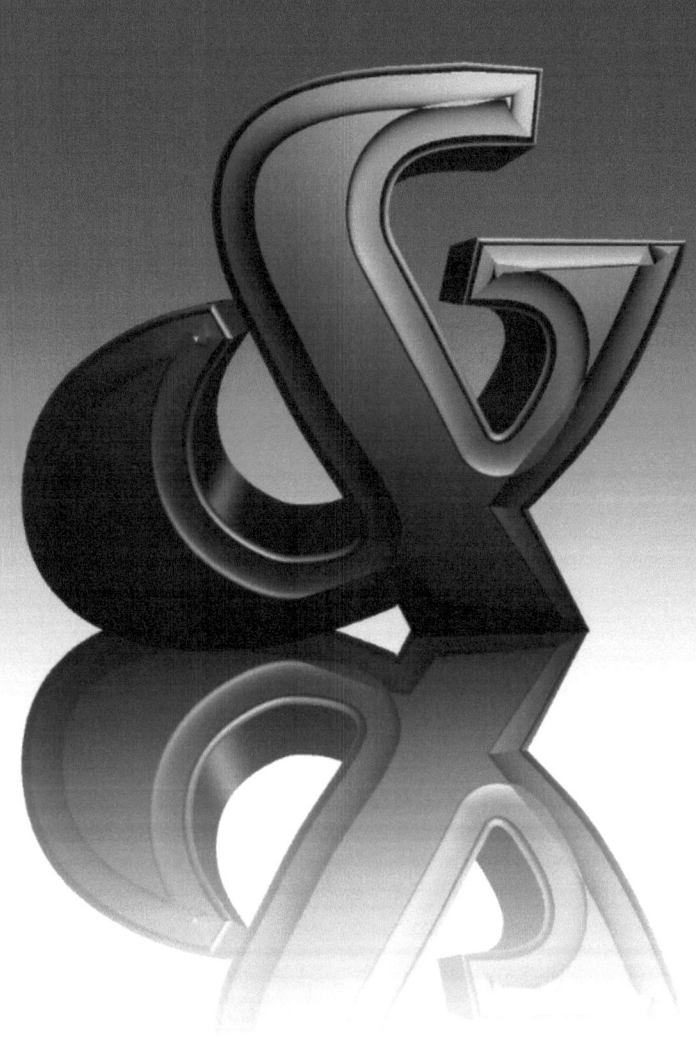

# PROFILE

MAKES THE MAN | A KINKED SERIES

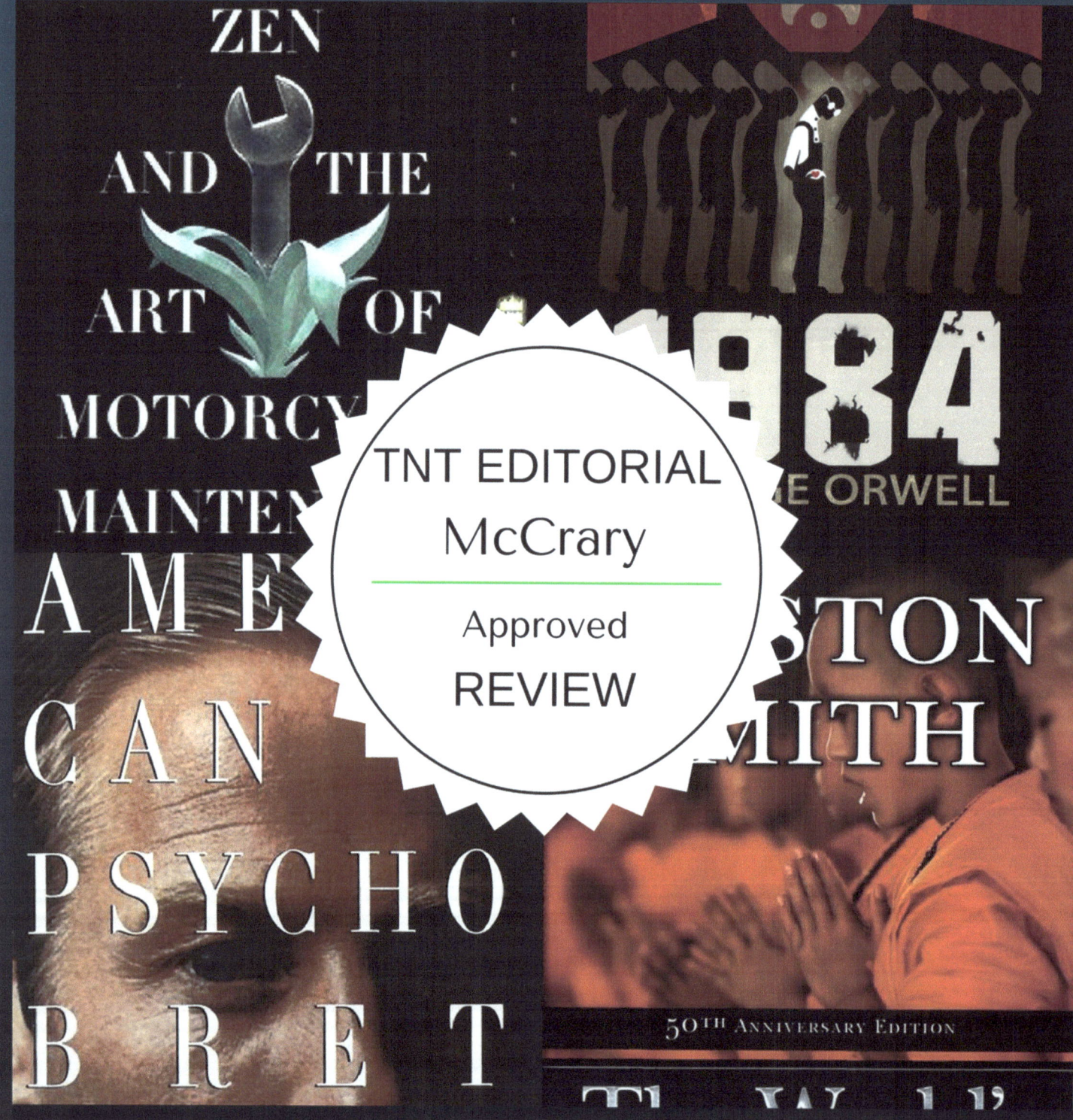

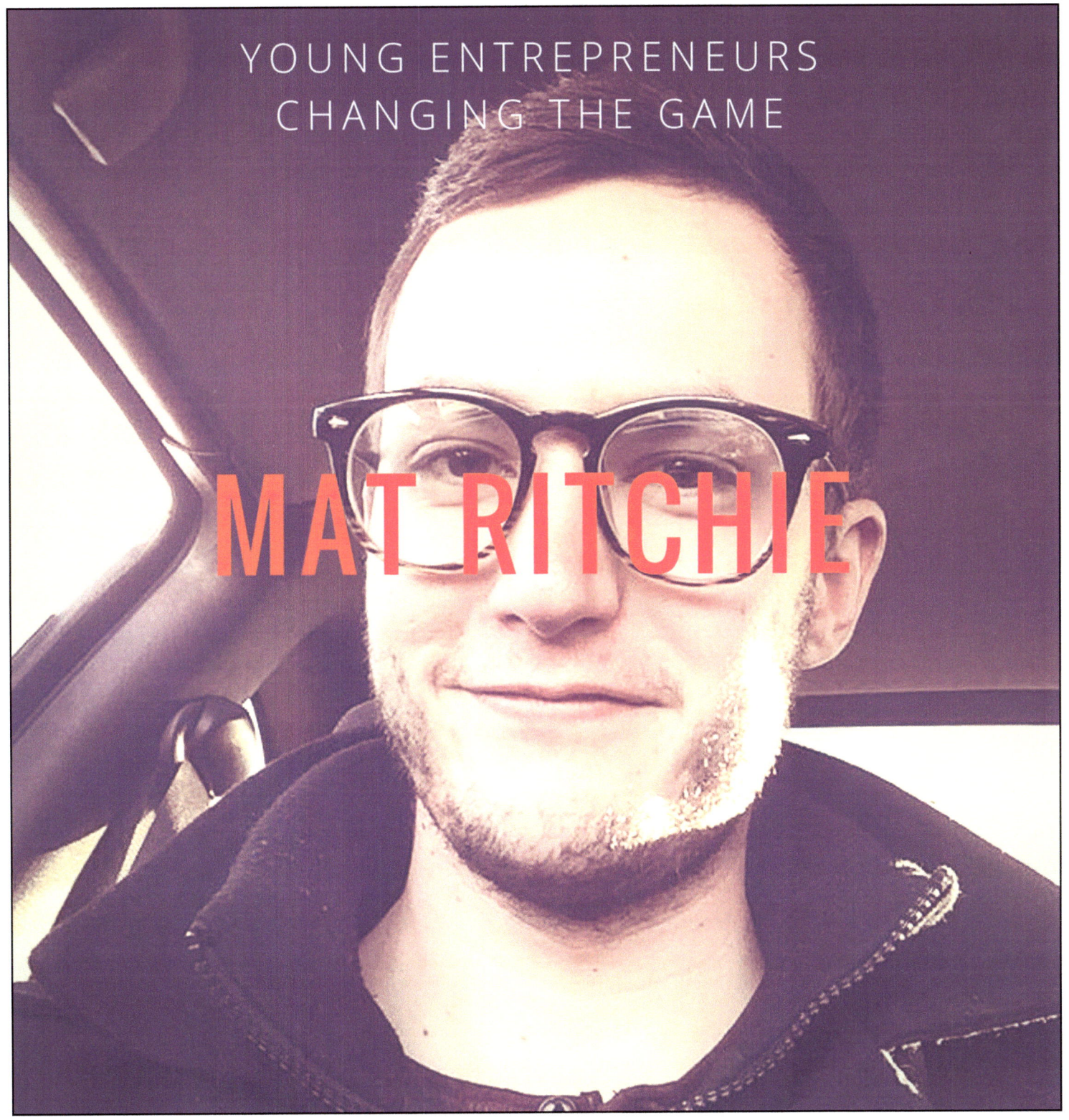

YOUNG ENTREPRENEURS
CHANGING THE GAME

MAT RITCHIE

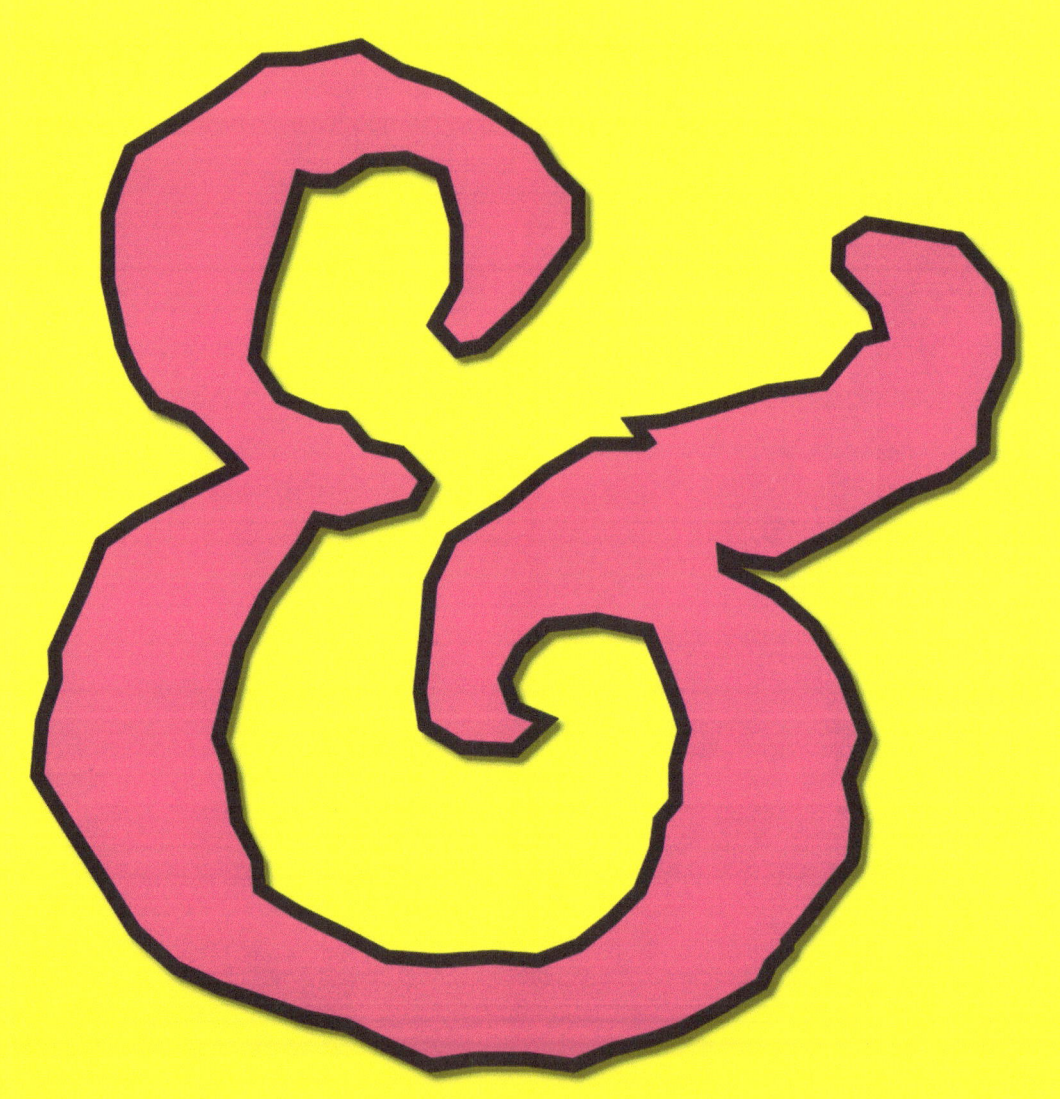

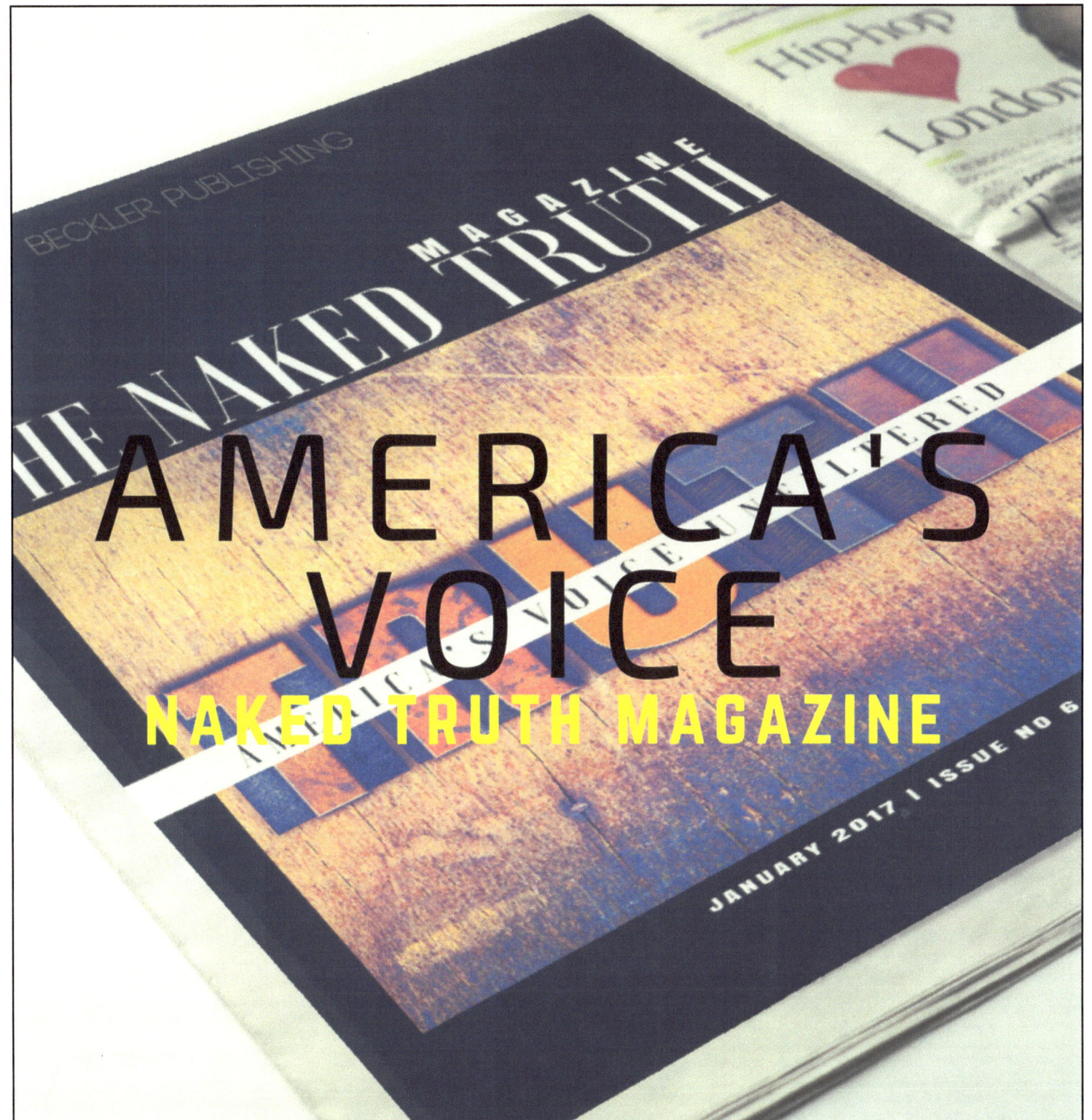

# TNT

## MAGAZINE

# The October Issue is Here!

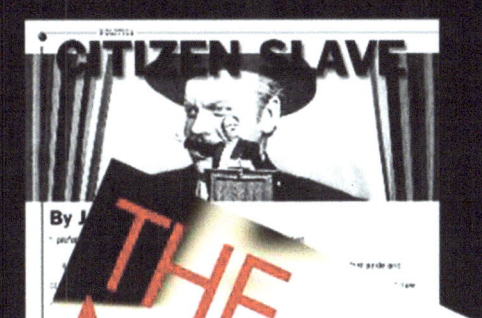

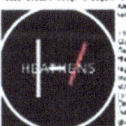

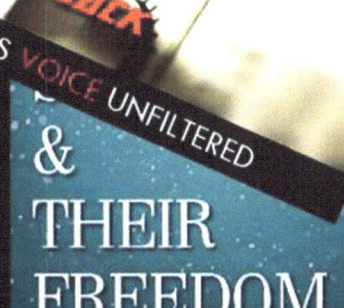
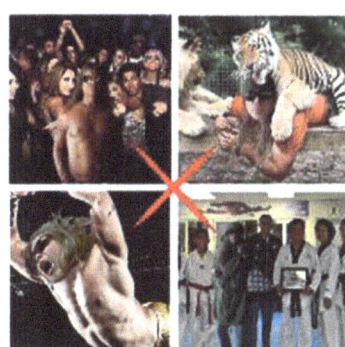

# Get Your Copy Today!

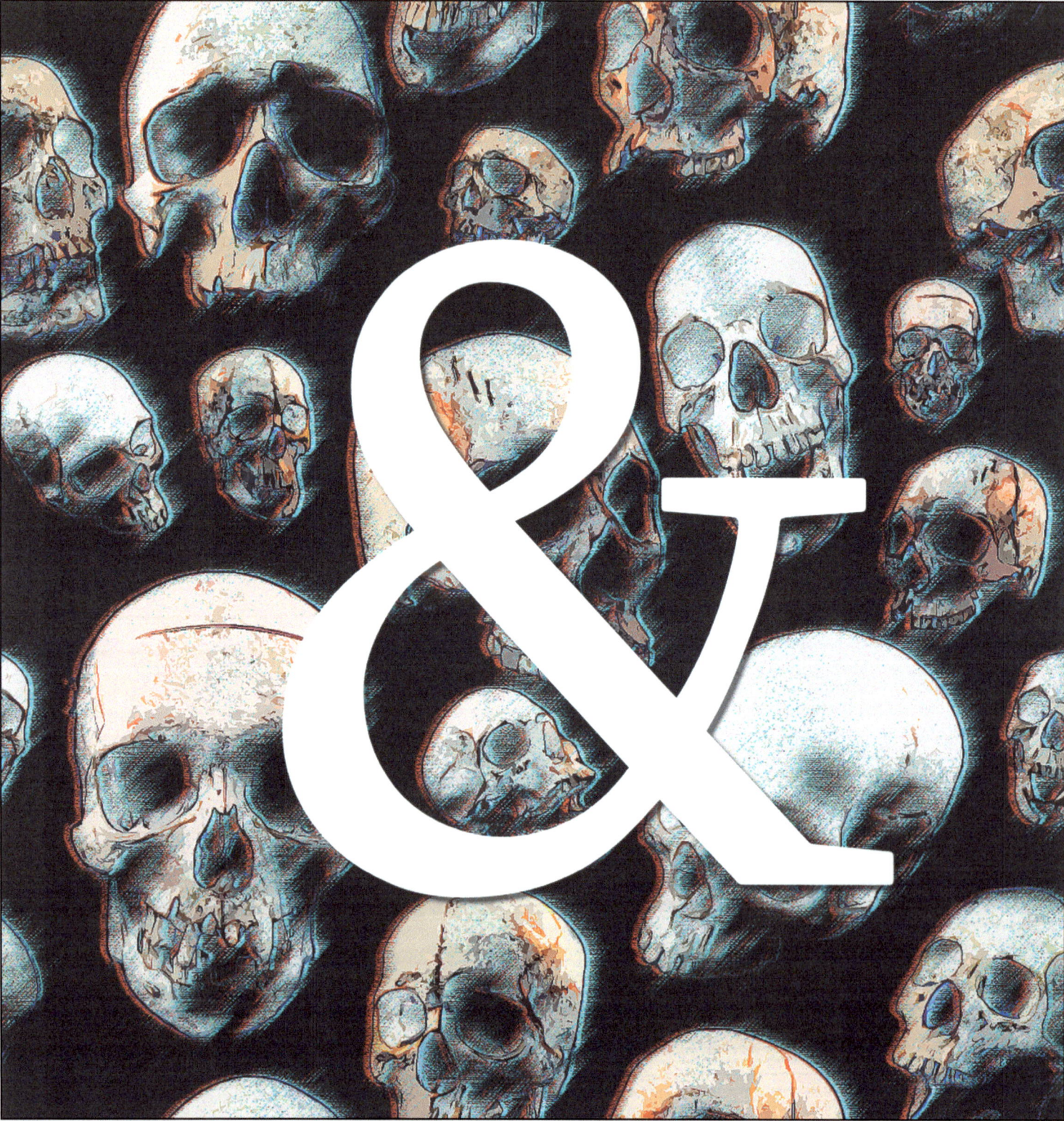

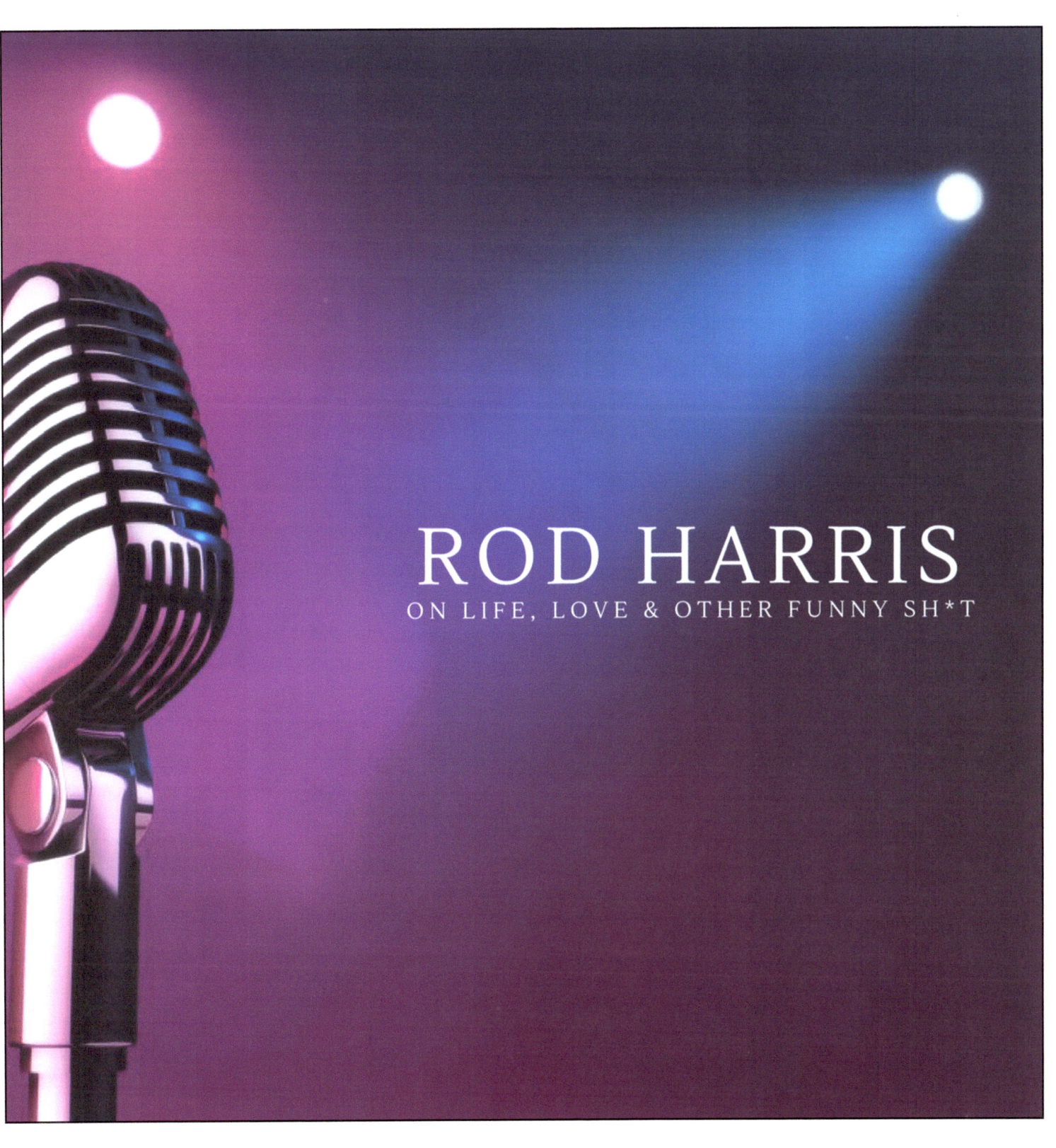

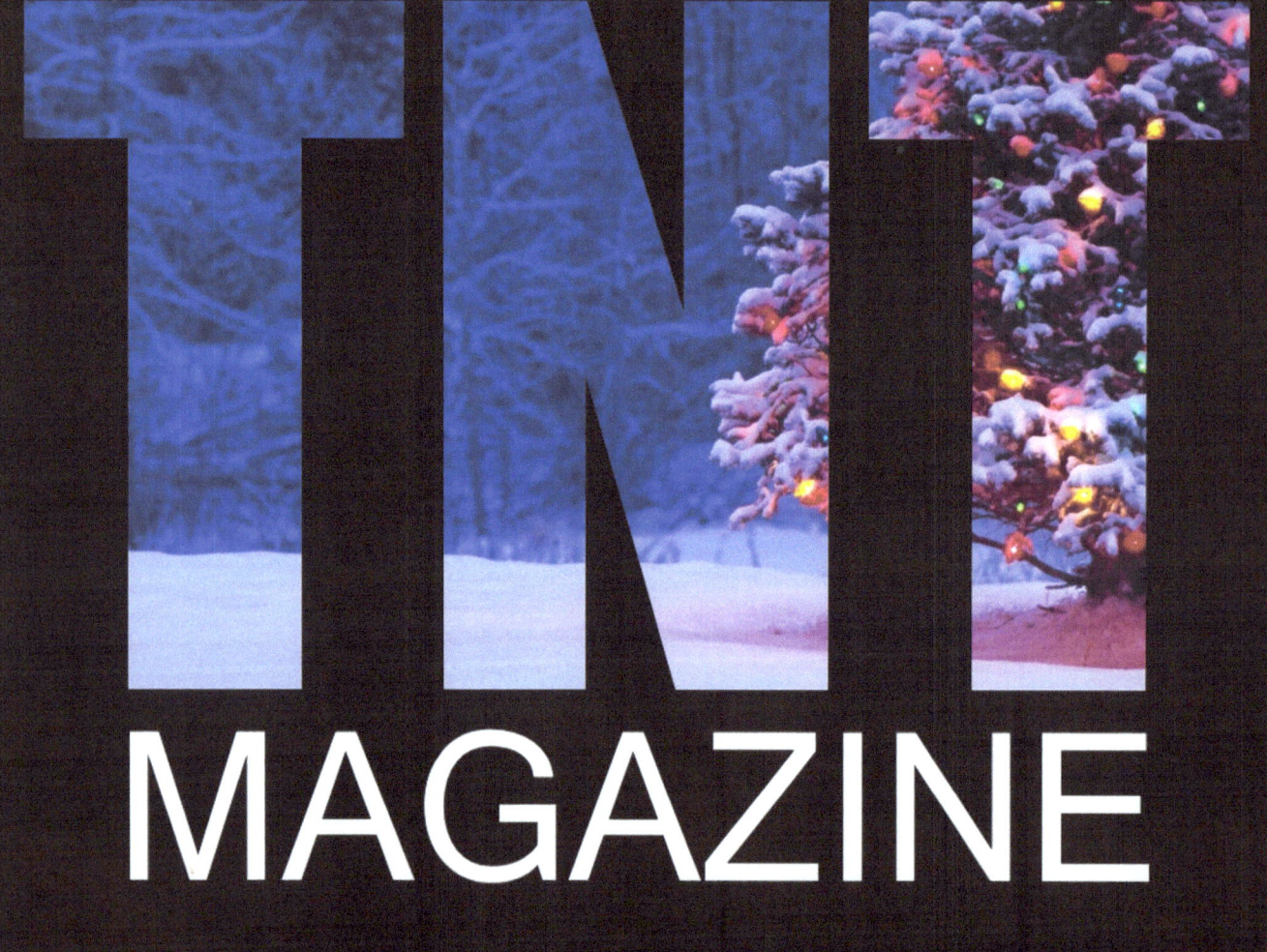

# TNT MAGAZINE

Merry Christmas

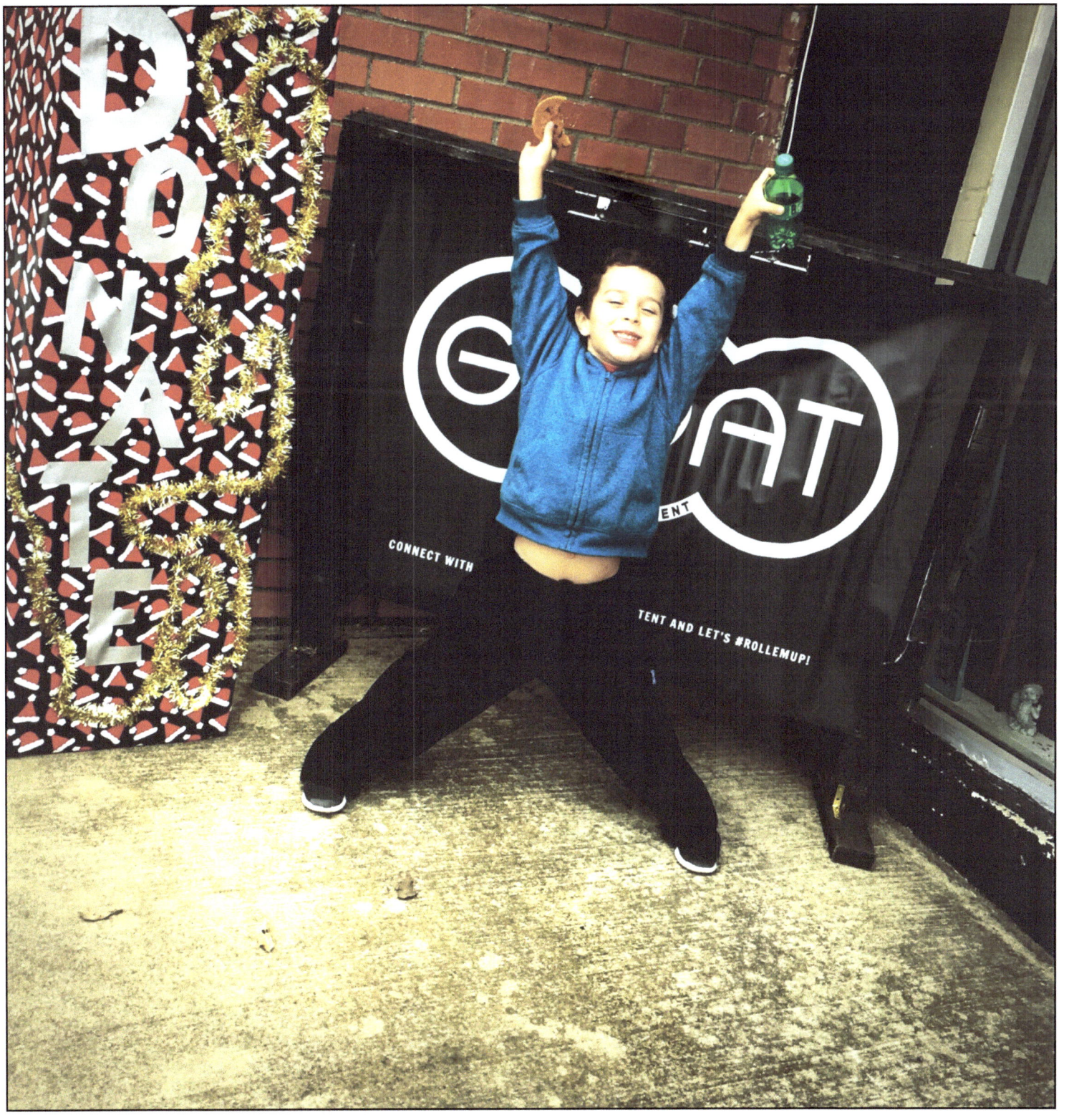

www.ingramcontent.com/pod-product-compliance
Lightning Source LLC
Chambersburg PA
CBHW051050180526
45172CB00002B/576